It Often Deprives Me of My Sleep

C.B. Publishing

Published by C.B. Publishing Company

Memphis, TN. 38125 U.S.A.

Copyright 2007 by Christopher D. Burns

Publisher's Note

Please visit: http://www.cbpublish.com

ISBN 0-9701952-8-1

13 Digit 978-0-9701952-8-9

Cover Design © 2007

It Often Deprives Me of My Sleep

Christopher D. Burns

Table of Contents

Intro

I've noticed, often, when words arrive in your mind and become an active part of your world that those words don't always have the same meaning that you gave them. A dynamic sequence occurs when someone reads words that held great value for you. A legalized rape, if you will, of the writer's mind. A malevolent entry into what you assumed was good. The odd thing is they never get what you are saying, but they can always do it better. Funny isn't it? Funny indeed. This business, this story, this way of life is not to be taken lightly, for each word placed on paper should be important in one way or another.

Begin

At what point does the story tell you when to write? At what minute does it awaken you and make you place words on crumpled pieces of paper stuck to the nightstand beside your bed? Leaning back in my chair and contemplating the research and the time placed into attempting this, forces me to hold my hands steady over each key. This helps me to succeed at one thing.

Anyway, as the monitor reflected onto my lenses, it seemed to be a righteous concept, until I found that I couldn't stand watching the videos. Those "Eyes on the Prize" and "Ethnic Notions," movies buried deep in the library under *Instructional Aids*. I couldn't finish any of them. The black and white newscasts that air on PBS every year. I couldn't make it through one viewing without lowering my head, closing my eyes and wincing at blow after remorseless blow.

Reading the narratives and speaking to the professors should have been enough to complete the task at hand. My task, an attempt at understanding society through stories. Fictional representations of the past. Instead, I had to watch the videos, and I became angry. If time heals all wounds, then time must be the true savior? If time truly heals, why do I cry so much every February?

I can't watch police pull pieces of skin

from swinging clubs, that battered and bruised us.

I can't watch the fire hoses as they spray.

I can't watch as dogs streak like gray flashes

across the screen, to attack the familiar

Black images that look like the puppets

the dogs were trained to kill. Black, gray and white

images ingrained, like dreams in my mind.

As blood sprays gray, hues deceive the viewer.

Videos recreate that southern state.

The four little girls from Alabama,

the Mississippi three slain for the cause.

The Arkansas twelve. Lonely, Ernest Green

held the torch for the numbers who believed.

I can't watch Black and White try to conceal

uncivil acts; how the right and left, left us.

These tears that burn my eyes come from my soul.

I became angry enough to continue. Angry enough to sit with my back tense from hours of hunched-over writing and typing. A wicked pain shooting up the side of my spine reminding me of the hours that I had shared with this obsession, this passion, this love. So I sat in front of the monitor and stared blankly at the empty page. I attempted to capture the essence of the foundation of this story; but new accounts of escapes to freedom are always hindered by the voice. Is that voice an uneducated soul finding their way? Is that voice a soul bound and shackled by the knowledge they can't share, or is that voice a spirit carried by the never ending desire to be free?

A slave's journal

Thick mud covers my ankles as I trods through this forests in search of freedom. Step after step, I attempts to slosh through the muck quietly, twigs and old leaves crumple and break under the weight of my gashed, bloodied feet. I wants to shout out and cry, but beyond them trees there lies a pain more cruel than open cuts on feet, there is the reality of being captured.

Thankful for the mud, I kneels into the soggy grass and scrapes the dew from the ground. I licks my hands hoping to get relief for my throat, which done swelled from the noose I escaped. I don't know what this road got in store for me, but the dawn mean that it's time for me to take cover. I attempts to find rhythm in a body that's been beat down by cowhide rules. Breathin produce knives shootin through the stings and burns of open wounds. Blood pumps from gashes every time I inhale and exhale. I still dreams about death, and desires to be hung and shot.

Runaway, Runaway, Done seen too many thangs; the Lawd , the Lawd done let me see too many thangs.

I'm finding hope in hearing bout freedom and what it's like.

Help me heal Lawd, remove these scars, remove these scars....

Can't sleep on my back cause the leaves and sticks break open scabs, leaving trails of blood. Ghost in they minds, and invisible; hiding in ditches, under molehills, by riverbanks, in the forests or in fields. Safety come with clouded vision,

I don't want nothing, but to be free. Free Lawd, I just wants to be free;

but I never can be, the plantation gave me an identity; but being free done created invisibility.

Damn, if this story needs to be told then why doesn't it flow? I can't comprehend at times if this is my job. Do I allow this fear of failure to possess me and scare me away? There is the constant feeling that I'm being watched by that narrator who strung the lights in his basement dwelling. Each block forces me to search inside the computer for a button to stop that damn cursor from flashing. If frustration is the beginning of inspiration then it seems that I'm inspired to place this story on the top of my printer until it regains whatever value I gave it initially.

Tell my story, one of dreams, silent sounds,
shifting melodies casting shadows of
our past. Tell our story of misunderstood
choruses sung in fields on plantations.
Tell my story, if you love who you are.

I love who I am, but I also despise who I am, at times.

Have you ever heard "Blue Train" follow Heron while thoughts of "Darn that Dream" linger in your brain? I have sat through the same series of CD's for hours. Listening to every flat note that, slowly becomes a brilliant piece of sound and texture after the seconds turn into minutes. Have you ever become lost in the thumping rhythm of "Cherish the Day," while contemplating if what you are creating is actually worth anything?

I have, while sitting at this machine manipulating the keys hoping to put this story to sleep by doing what it desires. I'll tell the story. I'll answer the questions and pray that someone cares. But if no one pays any attention, aren't my efforts useless? Is it the inevitable goal of an artist to find meaning in the senseless acts that occur? Well, actually the goal is to entertain, right? Uncertainty is a flaw that can lead to shortcomings, unfinished tales and tons of incomplete manuscripts.

And you're a writer?

I am.

Yet I find it impossible to tell this story. Why should I be designated as the Great Black Hope. It is beyond my comprehension as to why we don't have the privilege of anonymity. I can't be me. I can't write what I please because I have to write for you. I can't tell my story because I have to tell your story. If your story isn't told then I become an Uncle Tom, don't I?

And you're a writer?

I want to be, but I'm afraid of what they will say. If I tell the story am I destined to tell your story forever?

And you're,

I am.

I scratched a series of notes after reading a number of narratives that detailed the days that a slave endured. I even attempted to find meaning in what may have occurred. How is it that a man could have done those things to another man? Long before Schindler, did overseer's maintain a log?

Journal from the fields

August 29, 1864

The amount of indifference that floated through my head as I traveled through the plantation ensuring that my folks was completing their tasks for today, seemed minimal to the amount of hatred I hold for them. They don't deserve a place in my world, or deserve to be in the same sentence as man, woman or human. Beasts, the term I'd give them; along the lines of mules or oxen. The term slave is high praise. Fortunately, they can comprehend rules I established for them, which makes them acceptable.

September 2, 1864

The dust done become more of a problem as the harvesting season continued. It blew in from the old fields that no longer yielded cotton wanted by new businesses. The dust and heat become such a problem that I have to cover my mouth after drinking. Damn slaves tired quickly today. The sun was high and the wind was blowing. One boy, must've been about eleven years old, dropped down on all fours after sucking a lot of dust. His lips was cracked, hair plastered to his forehead with dirt and sweat. His back was as red as a hill of fire ants. Hell, he been working since well before the sun rose.

Along with twelve other little bastards in the field, and the parents, the thirty one slaves I was entrusted with seemed to be on they last legs.

The blood clotted in the corners of the boy's mouth. His parents wanted to help, but they knew better than to quit working. I rode over to where the boy fell and poured out my drink onto the ground next to him.

"If you get up boy and finish your work, you can lick that up," I laughed and watched the boy attempt to stand. His limbs shook as he placed one knee on the ground and pushed his way to his feet. He turned and looked at me as if he was bout to cry. He was so damned empty all he could do was make his chest heave.

"Boy you eying me? Get to work."

He moved slowly. Each stepped seemed to take as much effort as picking two bushels of cotton. The slower he moved, the more angry I got. My anger made me remove my thickest piece of cowhide from the holster. I cracked it into the air before it found its place on the boy's lower back. His skin ripped open and blood shot onto several rows of cotton.

Upon ripping into the child's back I yelled to the rest,

"If you feel tired, and you can't work, don't drop dead until the sun drops behind the edge of the trees and the sky hides your skin from my sight; or in God's name..."

December 25, 1864

I was the finest overseer this side of the Mississippi. In my life I found pleasure in most inhumane acts. Apologizing for what I do is not needed. This is who I am, this is who my people say I am, therefore I have no choice.

December 26, 1846

I had two try to escape today. Give the bastards an inch. Well, oddly enough after I draped the woman from an eight foot limb, that I'd used before, I found it easy to lay my cowhide into the back of the boy I found her with. I hadn't used my tools in almost four weeks. I must've whipped him for almost ten minutes. It was the first time I saw a man's ribcage through his back.

I tried to be easy, but they done tarnished my brass. I'll make them walk in the blistering, cold tomorrow and gather a hundred chords of wood for the Big House.

****

Where do I turn? If I say that I am, then why doesn't the story come to me?

In lyrics of songs, between the lines, outside of the truth, there is a story of a rebellion; but where does it end? Where does it begin? Where do I blur the line of reality and myths? If I can hear the story question my faith, then the story should hold out placards to guide.

There is a story of slaves and overseers. A fiction of escaping and actually being free. A great narrative of Haley's proportions but I can't handle the material. Maybe I'm too weak to speak out against how little we have changed.

I want to have that voice. A distinguishable sound that can provoke feelings through written words. Lord knows I don't want to spend hours at this computer expressing my loves, fears, desires, dreams, hopes, without ever sharing them with you. How can one claim to care for something that doesn't have any meaning? Why write if it doesn't serve a purpose?

We are a young generation. People expect us to do nothing and when we do something, it comes as a fantastic surprise. Has anyone ever really listened to our music. As much as I love Trane, I also love Hip Hop. I fear that this voice I seek will overshadow what I have to say. Young writers are rarely accepted, especially if they fail to write about popular topics. Yes, I do fear what has to be done with this, but I also fear a future where our greatest young minds are placed in jail, killed or whitewashed to the point where they honestly believe things have changed enough. I may not be able to watch the videos without turning my head at times, or finish narratives that explain in great detail who we are, but I can find a story within myself. I can listen to the voice and let it guide me. I can listen to the voice tell me of hidden stories of slave revolutions.

Fields

Can you smell the smoke drifting overhead?
The fields consumed in red, fiery colors,
Heavy gray smoke filling the autumn sky.
Ash from burnt stalks settling on shoulders.

In fields, the sweat covers ears of corn.
Blood blankets trees on old tobacco roads.
Rows of cotton echo spirituals
of struggle and carrying heavy loads.

Can you smell the smoke drifting overhead?
Snatching the air from our souls as we breathe.
Rolling flames singeing green grass, burning homes,
Each spark following the first fires lead.

In fields, we stood and watched the smoke drift off,
we stood and stayed there until the last flame
consumed what held our souls from true freedom.
Can you see the smoke set free our names?

I can. In books of roots that move up from slavery, I can. I see the fields where you were when the break of morning shined upon you, and the last light of day, whether moon or sun, set as you still toiled. I hear the lies and the stories, the deceit in the horns, "Bee Dee beee doo dow, dun, dun." Screaming horns, whistling madness, angry booms from sticks pounding percussive devices. I can hear, I can hear, I can see. In visions, in dreams asleep with my head in books, at dinner with my lover, I can see. I can hear, but I can't continue without sympathy. Are you sympathetic?

Do I change my name to some African moniker? Change my religion to Islam and wear dashikis for you to give me the rest? A hypocrite can site a million verses and become respected in the eyes of his fellow man simply from standing on the balcony and pointing. I can write your story, and I can write our story, but we won't read it, so what's the point? Garvey wanted to go home, but home is war -torn. We aren't truly accepted at home, so we have to make the best of what we have, which isn't as bad as it could be. Oh, have I contradicted myself? No. Things aren't as good as they could be because we aren't willing to be one.

Where is my love going for what I long to complete? Three months, fifteen days, seven hours and fifty-four, fifty-five, fifty.... An unfinished product of several incomprehensible, eight and a half by eleven sheets that seem to make sense only to the narrator.

In darkness of night, we continued on.

On trails like tracks beneath stars we tarried.

Above ground, under God's care we persevered,

for freedom in some form of sanctuary.

So I continue on, although this feeling of accountability seems to be my motivation. If the idea is to be selfless in finding and understanding the history, then guilt should not be a factor. Yet, I sit here and rummage through tons of encyclopedia copies and web pages seeking information that will gain the attention of all people. Something so shocking that it will describe through a single page how truly devastating history has been. But if my only desire is to prove how thoroughly disgusting things were, isn't that really a bastardization of our situation?

History itself is dramatic enough to reveal its importance, without searching archives for stories that describe the life of a woman who murders her children. A woman who takes her flesh, which matured within her for months and slays her babies to establish how vile slavery was. Do I justify such an act by making my writing an academic, beautiful piece of mystery and intrigue? Or do I tell the truth and say,

That lady was wrong.

You write the story and tell what you feel is right.

Damn that dream. Isn't a story about a young slave who learns to read by giving poor white boys bread more positive? Or is that not enough to express our history?

Right the story. Write the story.

I'm beginning to understand the plight of the writer. Specifically my plight, my struggle, my song. I can begin a story, but if I don't say the right thing then I'm ostracized. I'm punished not by Whites, but by my own for not upholding the flag.

This story of slave rebellion, lost in historical facts that I can't suffer through without wanting to hurt every White person I see, is hindering my perception of the purpose of the art form. Am I not without fault? If I am pricked....

Hold all that you do up to a light and see if it meets everyone's standards, then question me. For you have not carried the torch either. I want to finish but I believe that a more efficient work could arrive from the present. I don't have to delve into our past to find hatred and injustice, for nothing has changed. But I really would like to write about the good things. I want everyone to laugh and understand that there is some happiness. However, you insist upon becoming the black and white images behind my closed lids and I can no longer stand the pressure. Even as I stare into the monitor and follow you, follow the rise and fall of letters forming words, forming sentences, forming paragraphs, creating pages, I realize that it isn't me that's placing this into the computer, it's you. An odd sort of possession, only to be exorcised by continuing until you have nothing left to say. So I'll sit here. I won't move. I'll sit here and take back my existence. I'll only write my stories, not yours.

Why are ye fearful, O ye of little faith?

I fear what will be said. I fear failure and I fear what we all fear.

In time the truth will come to light, but why allow time to forget the truths that will subside with the loss of the story?

I've put the story aside to better understand what I should do. To write fictitious passages based on historical facts that deal with slavery is not the way I want to discuss us. If it is the stories will, then I will write that story. But I would much rather find something pertinent to who we are know. I guess it may be my choice after all. I'll write what's comfortable to me, what I understand. Write what I know as I exist in this day of post civil rights initiatives. Calling upon the dream, it seems that the story wants to change. I know that I want to change the story, so guide me. Help me place into words the story that moves beyond that one month of the year, beyond the designated title placed upon us. From Harlem to South Central, riot to riot, do we understand what brought us here? What facilitated our "completed" journey? This false equality of ours only discussed when a man is shot forty-one times by those who protect and serve.

Ideas spoken on college campuses but never taken into the community. The son of the Reverend on the balcony, running for office seems to be a great step forward, but at times, to me, he seems to be a puppet, of what or whom I am unsure of. But we do have a lot of puppets, and that scares me.

The Last Thirty Five

The idea was to walk in rhythm, for a purpose,

following Dr. King to the promised land,

A slow stride to freedom.

The idea was to march to the chords

of music ringing out in dispute of wrongs that had occurred,

A slow march to freedom, A slow march to freedom.

What happened to our walks, what happened to our marches?

What happened to us?

Lack of trust?

Content with the times, we allowed ourselves to settle.

The idea was to march and walk our way to equality;

but what happened along the way?

64 killed the Hajj, but pacified us with the Civil Rights Act.

68 murdered Rex, so they confused us with the text that continued the war.

They drafted us to prevent the movement and it worked.

Rainbows pushed and Panthers attempted to rally,

but the numbers were tallied and we found that nothing had changed.

So we became frustrated and settled.

We settled for the Rev. On the Balcony, who survived, to guide us.

The idea was to walk in rhythm, the idea was to march to the chords...

Lack of focus,

Lack of desire?

We began to tire, the projects didn't seem so bad;

at least we could ride the bus.

Lack of trust?

Lack of trust. We yelled Geronimo and they placed him behind bars,

decapitated the Panther, and covered it with the price of gas; we sat on our ass.

They rewarded us, so we didn't fuss we could go to their colleges.

We let go of the struggle because it wasn't hip to be Black.

Being Brothers and Sisters didn't suit us,

So we called each other niggas, and Blaxploitation made that cool.

The idea was to find our freedom, the idea was to give us hope.

The reality was they gave us dope.

I believe I can fly.

Fly away, float away, we accepted that.

In fact, we turned our backs on Blacks and opened our arms to crack.

We inhaled and exhaled, the doors opened;

we had more jobs and the Reverend On the Balcony ran for office.

We forgot to address crack, and the lack of the Black family structure.

The idea was to find our dreams and so it seemed

that we had. Out of the projects a few of us moved,

Well we moving on up,

Up to what? Babies Daddies?

I know the Lord

and the Lord knows you, so what else is new?

When we became content, the government spent their time behind closed doors.

They devised and they schemed and came up with a theme

that would separate you and yours.

Destroy the Black man, better yet let him destroy himself.

Give him a taste of White, give him a taste of wealth.

Other Blacks will get jealous over there in the projects and this will perpetuate,

Blacks will waste their time on ain't no good men and other foolish debates.

They got rid of the Klan and brought in gangs, brothers in blue and red.

Claimed eracism, lied about sexism, switched to Semitism and blamed it on Muslims "rage."

But it wasn't rage, simply put it was wage, the minimum which we received.

The idea was to walk in rhythm, the idea was to march to the chords,

We shall overcome, we shall -

No longer a need for that song, no need for a struggle;

Shush up. We where we want to be, don't cause no trouble.

Black boy murdered in the projects, Black man murdered in Jasper,

and Black leaders are just like Casper.

Shush up. Don't cause no trouble, we where we wanna be.

I said don't cause no trouble boy, we where we wanna be.

      Why give me the story if you don't want the words to speak out? This is what you wanted, not me. I don't know any other way to put it down. I'm angry. The videos, the history books, the words from people who sat in, the words from brothers who stood up, the water from the hoses that blew us down, are all ingrained in my soul. How else do I write these words? How do I continue? How do I tell the truth without anger?

You tell the story, don't let it tell you.

Scribble the words on pads, add in pauses,

and descriptive phrases to express anger.

You tell the story, don't let the story tell you.

      And if the story is told then may I write my stories?

Harvesting in Jasper

Today I saw a verdict, and unconsciously I smiled. I felt relieved that he was guilty. I sat here, stared at this screen and thought of how justice had been served. Served in our favor for a change. Oddly enough my pride and The Dream possessed my hands and filled the screen, but my thoughts didn't seem to agree with how I felt. I felt sad. There was not a reason to celebrate. There was a reason to feel disgusted, to feel ashamed of people. I felt sad. In the amount of time it took for a person to walk in and greet someone, shake their hand and exchange names, a life was forever etched into this societies reality. A reality that grossly resembled history. A history that had indeed repeated itself.

My fear, finds its ground on dark Texas streets

where air constricts from ropes stretched tight like stems.

Lady Day sang of Strange Fruit years ago,

Yet, I revisit the scene still today.

> *Pastoral scene of the gallant south,*
> *The bulging eyes and the twisted mouth,*
> *Scent of magnolias, sweet and fresh,*
> *Then the sudden smell of burning flesh.*

Far removed from the cloak of giant trees,

the harvest takes place on dark, and dusty roads.

A man struggles to keep pace with a truck.

He fails and skips on jagged stones that scrape

his Black skin from his bones. Blood trails behind

the White truck that speeds for almost two miles.

A man harvested in Jasper today

slowly dies like strange fruit hung from limbs.

What do you write when nothing has been accomplished?

You write of hope, you understand that we have changed.

But it isn't us that needed to change it was them. And they still haven't changed.

But we have.

The screams overheard through the rustling leaves,

whistling of whips that slashed into me.

Ringing shots as I tried to run away.

Barking of dogs as I hid in the hay.

Clanging from chains, I did all of their jobs.

Silence of tears down my face as I sobbed.

Sounds of the past, seem too loud to ignore;

silenced by those dying, Black on Black war.

I found myself at a place where the road divided into two directions. One sign claimed to be the path to happiness, the other claimed to be the road to truth. Underneath each sign was a plaque that stated,

The path chosen was the only way to reach your destination. There was not an alternative once the drive began.

I sat at the path perplexed about which road to choose, listening to a rhetorical hook tell me that, *Lady Day and Coltrane can wash your troubles away.*

Do I Know You

As I walked one day with my proud African stride, a man in a car asked if I needed a ride.

I contemplated the question and responded with one of my own, "Why have you stopped your car while driving alone? Haven't you heard that we are savage, haven't you heard that we hate?"

With my last question came great debate. His first response was unclear but he soon explained, that he no longer felt hatred, he was no longer insane. He stated he had been wrong for so many years, he claimed he had no choice, no voice among his peers. I found this quite amusing that this man had no voice for it was he, not we, who always had freedom of course. So I asked him, "Why the sudden change of heart?"

He responded by saying he had to do his part.

"What part ?" I asked, with a smile and a stare, knowing exactly what to expect and what was in the air. With remorse in his voice and tears in his eyes he began by saying,

"For my people to rise...." He then stopped and looked at me close with his eyes straining and spectacles on his nose. "Do I... know you?" His voice trembled and shook.

"Oh yes," I stated and gave him a look. From where he knew me he had no reason to ask,

for it was at this point I removed my mask. What appeared to his face was enough to stop his heart, thank God it didn't for this was his final part.

I ripped off my shirt and began to change from the strong Black figure into something he at first found strange. My eyes became swollen, blood flowed from my depths, on my back appeared lashes from the right side to the left. I moved towards a tree and fell against the root

I took my place along the bottom like a piece of strange fruit. My voice grew heavy and I begin to sing, oh what pain and regret to the old man did I bring. He placed his head in his hands and began to cry, "Enough!"

I looked at him angrily, trying to be tough. I responded with an equally loud cry of my own, "There is no such thing as instant forgiveness, just pass this experience on." With those words I began walking again with my cool confident stride, until another car stopped. . .

"Hey man, need a ride?"

Hidden inside of numerous details of our past are stories of family, unity and love. Hidden within our stories today, there are people who strive to be Black. I find myself stuck between caring too much and not caring at all. Stuck between giving all that I have and giving only to those who I believe deserve it. Can a book full of personal words have an effect on anyone? Do songs really inspire someone to do the right thing?

The right thing is done when a person takes the words, the thoughts, the emotions and uses them.

But what I'm asking, I guess, is can a person be Black without really being Black? Their skin, dress, way of life can be African, but if they don't go out and physically help those whom they claim to be reaching, then isn't that person a hypocrite?

Will a dream die if the person having the dream dies?

Only if the person fails to share that dream.

Then indeed it is the way you teach and live, not just the way you live.

What have we become when we can't raise children who can distinguish between good and bad? Do we fault the children for not listening to us? Or do we understand that it isn't the fault of the child, but the fault of both.

Do As You're Told

As a child he was disciplined by many strict rules. His father prayed he wouldn't grow to be a fool. Dear old dad used to say, "Do as you're told!" His words came out clear and bold.

But the words he spoke carried little weight, with his son who at the time was only eight.

Slowly, his little boy grew to be a young man, who had dreams of success and college plans.

Everything was in order or so it appeared. His son's life, was like a car that his father steered. Until one day his father made a wrong turn, and began teaching a lesson that would be unintentionally learned.

While the father sat in his room doing private things, a gift his loving son walked in to bring. The father who was startled by his son's entrance turned his back to his son who steadily advanced. The father shouted loudly, "Get out!" "Not now!"

"But dad," his son said with a sad look upon his brow.

His father responded, "Listen to me, do as you're told."

To his son who was now fifteen years old. His son being one who never disobeyed, picked up his gift and was on his way. When the son stopped to look back and question why?

He happened to catch a glimpse out the corner of his eye.

"Could it be, no way, not my dad."

But indeed it was, in his hand, his father had, a crystal clear, glistening beautiful pipe; filled with smoke which his dad inhaled with all of his might. With this scene of confusion fresh in the son's head. Down the stairs and out of the house the boy sped. As he wandered and ran all over town, he replayed his father's actions and what had just gone down. He came to the conclusion that it was okay, so he tried it also with no delay.

He pressed his lips upon the tube and slowly inhaled. He paused and looked away and with his arms he flailed. He began to run, to and fro, and didn't realize he was doing so.

He jumped up and down/off the curb and back on; and then began to cry for reasons unknown. Lost in a dream and high as a kite he climbed up a fire escape til he was far out of sight.

He soon reappeared with his arms outstretched truly a sight to behold. As he took flight like an eagle he heard the words, "Do as you're told, Do as you're told."

****

Here is what you desire. The story of us, but do you want to hear it? Do you want to hear our story? It isn't a story of slavery, it isn't a story of hate. It is a story of love and what happened to it.

If it was for me to guide then I have done my duty. I will follow you and be with you always.

Will I hear you when the monitor becomes blank and the words are lost inside the brightness of the screen? Will I have to await the words that will begin the next story, or do they all come from within now?

The stories have always come from within, you've finally listened.

What exactly does it mean to be a writer? Better yet, what does it mean to be a young Black writer? No matter what I write, I keep coming back to the fact that I am a Black writer. Someone told me the other day that,

"The page is white the letters are black. The identity is somewhere in between."

But that isn't true, is it? Can I find my anonymity in the pages I create? Can I become just a person who loves to write, between these pages. Am I allowed to shirk my responsibility as long as I am hidden by pseudonyms and alter egos? Can I write poetry and stories combining them if I choose or am I bound to a code of ethics?

Find a way to tell how you feel. Have pride in who you are and question only that which is worthy of questioning.

I realize that we're the way we are because we don't see what we do to each other. If we gave a damn about anything we would see the things that we do to ourselves. It used to be that we could place blame for every Black death on circumstances beyond us. Now we're afraid to accept that often it is us who has done the most damage to us. Even the instances where things have become brutal from the hands of other races, are often dwarfed by the ugly deeds that we continue to commit against one another...

Ignorance begins the delusion.
Knowledge brings it to a conclusion.
Is peace forever an illusion,
due to our social confusion?

Jay's Corner

Jay threw his sign at the car that rolled by,
And took a drink from his brown paper bag.
He rolled a joint and began to get high,
A daily routine for this kid who sagged.

Above the law unafraid to meet death,
Immune to truth due to media views.
Refused to study to be like the rest,
At fifteen he killed for his blue tattoo.

The kid he murdered had straight A's in school,
He lost his life for no reason at all.
Jay laughed about it thinking it was cool,
The dead kid's brother wanted Jay to fall.

The lights shut off as the vehicle sped,
Too high to escape, from six wounds, Jay bled.

How did we move from street football to street wars?

Not Too Long Ago

"Car time," Willie called, as the heavy, green Delta 88 floated around the corner over patches of black asphalt mixed with old concrete. All the fellas ran to the side of the street and stood, breathing heavily. Tony held the football in his right hand tossed it back and forth in the air. He was the best at everything, the best quarterback, point guard and believe it or not he was the best student too. We were all pretty smart, but he just seemed to be a little better. The green bucket finally passed us and we got our game going again. Third down and my team had about two street lights to go before we scored. I was glad Tony and I were on the same team. We formed a huddle and Tony called the play. "Statue of Liberty. Willie, come behind me and take the ball. Throw the ball as soon as you take it and I'll go long." Day after day, we did the same thing, according to the month. Summer was like that. The first month of summer break was football. The second month was basketball, which I liked the most. I liked hanging the crate on the telephone pole after Fat Freddy broke the bottom out of it. I was always Sidney Moncrief. Tony had to be Jamaal Wilkes, always the best.

The third month was anything goes since school was about to start. Our neighborhood, our street, always played Greenlawn. They were the closest street to ours, without really being in our neighborhood. The games were great. I think we must have gone through several crates on some days. Our halftimes spent running to the candylady. Sucking Lemonheads and drinking Jungle Juice was our refreshments. Big Head was the entertainment. He had this giant boombox that he always played Run DMC on, "I'm the King of Rock, there is none higher. Sucker MC's should call me sire." That was our call. We were the street to beat, but things changed as we grew. We stop playing street football. Atari came out, and instead of Jungle Juice and basketball, we played Jungle Hunt and Frogger. We didn't see Greenlawn on our street unless somebody had beef. Things changed. Fat Freddy moved to another part of the city and Big Head had discovered NWA. We were older. Tony and I still hung tight except now I was Bernard King and he insisted on going backwards, he was Clyde Frazier. My boy. Ton had the sweetest between the legs dribble, and his defense, damn. He could stop a mack truck from getting to the hole. He always told me, "Don't bring your feet to close together. Watch his hips man, his hips can't fool you. Just watch his hips and slide your feet."

Sometimes Ton and I would play ball until our legs shook from weariness. I still remember the good times but it hurts to know that I made it to college as a ball player and Tony continued with his studies. That was all he could do. Have you ever found life to be so ironic that at times it seems as if the world only allows the bad things to happen to you? I have, but it wasn't until I truly understood what real happiness consisted of, when things began to change. Tony didn't have to play ball. True enough, he did enjoy it, but he didn't have to play. I still speak to him although I'm over two-thousand miles away. His voice is still strong and full of joy. A man like Tony never let a sport make him who he was. He made himself who he was by remaining faithful and forgiving.

I'm who I am because I've found that the only way to live is to live trying not to regret. I live for Tony. Every hoop I make, every between the leg dribble, every charge I take, is for Tony. I write this for Tony.

Is it easier to write what you know, or to create a story. It seems that there are a million stories to tell. But do I speak for everyone? Can I cross those barriers, color, status?

A story is universal as long as it is told well.

Universal? Is every story universal? Do we all have the same dreams? To rise up from slavery, to be loved for who we are, to cure invisibility, is that universal? How can a person understand that which wasn't in their ancestry? How do I understand that which I haven't lived through? I understand because I'm still called nigger. But what makes me angry is that I'm called that by my own more than I am by any other race.

I found that the moment when the words fail to make any sense and when they stop coming to you altogether divorce the work, grab the closest piece of anything that will help you forget the work and use it.

There is a time and place for everything, and I'm trying to find that place where things are that way. I'm seeking that place where we really do have a time, and a place to do everything. I long to find what will repair us. I pray that words do make a difference. I sincerely hope that this story will finish itself, instead of finding it's way into the unfinished folder on the desktop of my computer. But I know that it will never reach you and the dream will resurface and inspire me to speak again of things which I fear.

I'll write thousands of sentences, attempting to maintain the point of view, attempting to establish plot and conflict. Trying to create a setting which everyone will understand, and I'll spend years hoping to be a successful writer. All the while I'll be losing jobs and lovers who can't deal with the mood swings and late nights of fingertips striking keys that resound like rapid fire in the latest street war. This life will leave me alone and penniless only to find my greatest success after I'm gone. The only thing is, will anyone truly understand our plight? If they do, then that is enough, isn't it?

What I fear the most is never finding another love. A love which loves me as much as I would love... What seems awkward is that I seem to be caught behind myths and legends of who Black men are. Lies, some truths, of what Black men do. It used to be that we were too savage. We, broke down by the whip, the burden of being men without a home. A floating history of not being able to love which, like a hellish dark, red storm cloud, has followed us for centuries. A history now reinforced by our own actions and thoroughly enforced by books that sweat it out until they breath freely. Do we have any support at all? Or do I continuously find myself awaiting destiny's soulmate?

If it is love that you desire look within and your beauty will be undeniable. I value what you are attempting. Someone will love you. Just because she left, don't let go of your dreams.

But people don't believe that we hurt, that when it ends we don't sit and shed tears, wonder if we did enough. No one seems to care that I long to find peace.

The End

The smiles shared for years, the first hug,

the first kiss, awkward and too fast,

can't be removed in a day.

Yet the love that has faded,

from misunderstandings and lack of

conversation, continues to lock you

into the world you created with her.

Her eyes, once an escape from sadness which

removed frustration and anger, no longer

soothe and calm.

Now that you've grown apart

and moved away from her,

to recall her eyes creates pools within yours.

When do you leave behind a love that bound

you to a soul that made the heaven

in your dreams real?

Do you leave when you can no longer stand

her presence?

Do you leave when she won't accept the

faults that inherently belong to you?

You still love her, because she was the first

and you don't know how it's supposed to end.

You don't know how to let go, you don't know how.

I can't continue until I forget her. All that I want to accomplish seems small compared to this pain I feel. Are men suppose to share these thoughts? Does stating this help me to find my path and continue with my task? I guess it doesn't matter, you know? Everything is relative. But was it really me that was wrong?

Calm madness, quiet anger

frustration, sadness, hate and

loneliness; I can't believe

I, so foolish, so foolish.

Holding on to the hope that

she matures; that she evolves.

Wanting to find happiness,

simple desires to be loved,

unfulfilled aspirations,

I can't hold it together.

I, so foolish, so foolish.

Damn, why can't I write anything. This shit, damn it, damn it all. Who are my fingers trying to reach, who? Who fucking cares, not one fucking person cares. I could write until my fingers bleed and no one would ever fucking care, no one. Who cares if I write-

Write, I care.

How can it be that a story that once had such great potential become maligned? How do you move from issues that are pertinent to us, to something that only happens to you? Is this what life is all about? Love losts, love found, love, love, love, love. One continuous heartbreak after another. A life lived in a crystal shell, hanging from a line that is only as strong as the time you place into weaving it. But who gives and who receives? Was Romeo and Juliet really the greatest love story because of love? Or was it a great story because of sacrifice?

There is something that can be said of a man who understands.

What?

A man who understands, knows when to admit that he was wrong. He knows when it is time to move on, he knows when it is right and when it's time to slow down.

I sat there staring at my hands. The slice across the knuckle of my forefinger opened with every tap of the keyboard. The stitches attempting to hold the two flaps of skin together poked out beneath the heavy band aid on my right hand. My hand throbbed as I continued to type. Regardless of the pain, I had to finish the last few sentences that sat in my thoughts. Every thought about her infuriated me with such anger that I realized that it was probably hurting me more than it was hurting her. She probably hadn't thought about me at all. But I continued to write. My brain pounding behind my eyes. Every time I move my head, the blood rushes to a vacant spot in a location that causes me to blink. Do I hate her? I don't know if I do, but I do know that she has caused me to fail at furthering what I assumed would be that book that would help me establish who I was. But who am I really? Who are we?

A people.

Are we a culture? How can we be if we don't know of our history before the middle passage? We are so confused. I am so confused.

Ode to R.W.E.

To be what I am is my decision. At times it is the decision of others. What am I you ask? I am invisible. Not invisible because of an experiment gone astray. I am unseen because my color brings to mind the darkness of your hearts who want to control me. My hair, symbolic of tangled chains and shackles which once bound me on the chain gangs, but now links me to your future. The blood flowing from my wounds represent the hope and dreams that are removed from my grasp. Control me! You may try to control me but there is no way that you can. I have been through hell and I still exist. My existence I compare to picking the leaves of a daisy in a game of she loves me, she loves me not. Except there is no love involved, only deceit and the will to dominate. Through it all I have persevered while in seclusion. But my disappearance from society is only temporary, for I feel it is shameful to hide from fate. A fate designed for us. What I have learned may prevent what awaits people such as myself. My knowledge of invisibility can help me control my fate. I now understand that in a blink of an eye I can disappear and reappear, only to find that nothing has changed in front of me, but at the same time things can change.

Although my life has been a bleak existence of, "Coulda, shoulda, and woulda," I feel it is my duty to change this by using my experiences to help myself and you as well. To help you deal with the people in our society that think we are better off, in their eyes, unseen.

Baldwin, Hughes, what did they know? Walker, what does she know? What is it that they understood, what they understand? Did they realize that society only accepts stereotypical aspects of certain people? Or did they find that only after a person accepts that anyone can become invisible, then that person can control, understand and adjust to their situations?

Why did it take me so long to realize that you shouldn't have to experience an overabundance of hardships before you learn that you are only as valuable as you allow yourself to be, not as society allows you to be. Sometimes I dream of what things would have been like if only our leaders had lived. Speaker of the house, El Hajj Malik Shabazz. Former governor of Mississippi, Mr. Evers. What a country this could have been. Then again what a country this is, don't you think?

America.

I am swimming in a sea of shallow dreams, but I'm afraid to stand and walk to them. I feel the pressure of society, but it is light compared to the weight I place upon myself. I am constantly being told that I appear anxious. Many times I have internally lashed out at those who have told me this. Maybe because they are right. I am anxious, but if you were me wouldn't you be? I'm sure you would. If you don't think so you may be in a state of denial. When you first see me you expect me to be a certain way. I have come to find out that no matter how liberal people are, we all shake hands with the right. Our opinions are all under the influence of the media drug. We have been so heavily sedated that only a few truly understand how life was meant to be. Those people have no prejudices, no petty quarrels. They only care about being fed. But how soon will they too be under the influence? How much time will pass before they are being raised and fed this dope. Brokaw at six o' clock sharp. Walters with the interview of a lifetime. Slight paranoia isn't a bad thing, it keeps you on your toes. Where am I going with this? No where.

Have you ever tried to pry your five fingered vein from the remote control needle that transports the electronic dope from the pushers of media horse? Or if you choose you can ride these White horses into... By not clicking on you have to access knowledge through other sources.

If you aren't aware the net was made to kill the library.

The amount of research it takes to write a book of some substance isn't as easy as pointing and clicking your way to your own web page. The death of the library is the death of America. Words destroy us, build us, cause us to smile, and to be angered. Words give us life, hope and breath, written words. Words that you can feel on paper. Words that can be read by candlelight to a friend, a lover; family. The death of the book, is death.

A slave's journal

Done found freedom, done found it. But I done leff behind family. Missin them badly. It ain't so bad, jus lonely. White folks still looks at me like a nigger up here. They jus don't say it. They jus looks.

Conflict, words in stone, etched into our soul.

Attempt to express all things you behold.

I'm at the end of my rope. Trying to maintain control of my life is hard. I can't stand to see her. It becomes an interruption. But I have begun to step away from it. I can understand why the time it takes to complete anything is always hindered by thoughts of past loves. The whole thing makes me bitter. Yesterday I was rummaging through my desk, as I tried to pick things up. I sat and took a breath. I searched for old quotes and papers. Something to fill in the space. Something to get me started. To place this square through the right hole, instead of allowing my perception to deceive me.

The Notes

I hid the notes today as I cleaned the house.

I hoped that would help, and I feel that it did.

But is it for me to hide the notes,

or should I just allow them to be seen?

I can't stand seeing them because they lie.

They claim honesty and sincerity, but they lie.

Only words folded on a sheet of paper,

but they are so much more.

Flowers are temporary;

symbols of love last only as long as the moment.

Words last forever, for all to see.

I hid the letters today,

but they are still there in the place that I hid them.

Waiting to be read, waiting to be held, waiting to be loved.

I can remember what the letters said, but it doesn't matter.

The person who wrote them doesn't remember any of them.

I remember them all;

each individual piece of white,

twenty-four line,

red margin on the left hand side, paper.

One, in particular missing a comma.

I had written too much. Too much about her. I couldn't believe that my time had been so occupied. I spun in my chair with my back to the computer. I stared at the TV, and listened to "Embrya," it didn't help. My chair made indentations in the heavy, brown carpet. From the light coming in the window, I could see dust particles floating in the room. The dust settled on a vase full of potpourri, which no longer smelled the same. I walked over, sat on the floor and moved my chess pieces around. Lonely. The breeze caused the blinds to clap together. From the top of the entertainment system dust followed the light throughout the house, as far as the wind could push it and then,

The Balloon

The balloon fell.

My heart fluttered as the wind pushed it off of the pedestal I placed it upon.

For me to have kept it was a mistake in the first place.

Maybe it was fear?

Loneliness can create such turmoil,

that it becomes sad when the heart fails to move on.

As hard as I try, the pain becomes more pertinent.

Only when the emotions encounter new feelings

are they inclined to find peace.

Still the question remains,

when the balloon fell off of its pedestal today,

was it intentional or was it just wishful thinking?

I am sad.

I don't know if I still love, but I do know that I'm sad.

I wish I could remove the balloon,

but even with it gone I can still see it.

Sitting upon the pedestal; smiling and knowing that it has me spellbound.

Content in late night calls that bring me to my knees

I fear that I am the only one who hears the whistle

as the air escapes from the balloon.

Escape is always a consideration when I sit in front of the keyboard. But I have never made it past the guard. This muse that holds me, keeps me warm, keeps me sane. Allows me to pass, but I fear leaving her grasp. If I decide to walk away then I have failed. And just as I'm afraid of never finding love, I'm equally afraid of giving up on my dream. I guess this is a common phobia that afflicts us all, but I can't get over mine. So I will write. I will reminisce. Creating stories that confront the things that make me shudder, the things that make me feel something. I'll live inside my world taking everything for what it is. Not believing what my eyes take in as beautiful, only accepting what my heart believes is honest. I will get over her in time. I will get over us in time, but I will always remember her.

I've always wanted to question other men about how long it took them to get over her, the first love.

When I First Met You

Her beauty overwhelmed me and left me at a loss for words. I saw her from a distance. When our eyes met, temporarily I felt at peace. I moved towards her praying that it was me she was smiling at. My heart pounded. My palms wet. I had contemplated for over an hour about approaching her. I wanted so badly to speak with her, to hear her say her name. To hear her state that she was waiting for me also. She continued to smile as I walked closer. My movements seemed awkward and uncomfortable. The grass under my feet cushioned; making my journey seem effortless. I felt that I'd found something that had eluded me my whole life. Love at first sight, cliche? Happiness upon an initial glance was the truth. I found myself giggling and smiling like a child.

Emotions are the downfall of a man seeking fulfillment, emotions deceive.

I continued to walk gaining confidence with each step. Becoming a slave to my heart. Our eyes touched as I came face to face with her. We walked with each other and found that the shortest distance to love is friendship.

Friendship, next time I assume that I'll learn. The right decisions will be made. Soul and soma.

****

I was once told that happiness is a state of mind in which one forgets to be sad. But when I forget it seems that I only forget those things that make me smile.

You are failing to see everything. All that makes you feel anything other than pain is good.

How can that be? Just because you don't feel hurt of frustration that doesn't mean that you're happy.

It does. The irony of pessimism is in the decision to be a pessimist. You can always continue if you ask yourself this simple question, If your desire is to express a certain truth then who is stopping you?

I suppose I stop myself. I forget to make the most of my time and of my imagination. I want to write of happiness. I need to write of cliches', blue skies, sunshine, pizza on Friday night with the fellas, prom night and when I discovered you.

Kismet

Calm, close to shift change. I stood on the fantail staring at the waves, jumping and reaching for the rails of the ship. The sun fell over the horizon and sank into the ocean. I checked my tool pouch and pulled off my cranial. Ducking under the nose of one of our birds I stopped to take one more look at the sunset. Five and half months out at sea had given me a better appreciation of how small I was in comparison to everything else in the world. I stepped over several tiedown chains, which held the airplanes in place as we sped toward home. My boots clanged onto the metal steps as I jumped into the catwalk and entered through into the shop. The day had been hot, but regardless of the flight ops and the work that we continued to do although we were thousands of miles away from the Gulf, it didn't bother me at all. Two weeks from home I thought, two weeks from home. I had begun to dream about what I would do when I got back, where I would go.

After shift change the whole shop went down for chow. We talked and cracked on each other as usual and for the first time I was silent. Something was in my head. A voice, continuously laughing and repetitious in its refrain. It made me smile because I felt that everyone else could hear what was going on in my head. I left the galley and went back upstairs and got ready to shower.

Close to home, like a poem,

home is where the heart is.

I laughed. Lifting the top of my rack to grab a pair of underwear and the rest of my shower stuff made me think of the whole cruise. Damn, Singapore was a trip. I tried to think about every place I had seen but I couldn't focus.

Close to home, like a poem,

home is where the heart is.

I didn't realize what was taking place. I just continued with my routine. I never really paid any attention. I couldn't understand why my head was full of these things. Poems, stories, thoughts of the places I'd been, the things I'd seen, I couldn't understand and I ignored. Even as I arrived back to the States, floating underneath the Golden Gate Bridge with the December air creating white words on a cold silver morning canvas, I refused to hear you. The thousands of faces on the pier waving. Red, white and blue, flowers and I Love You Daddy banners, strung on ruffled, twisted pieces of paper created more noise in my head. Lovely noise, rather music and it was clear, the sound of it all. But I didn't listen, until now. You were speaking to me.

I was.

I know and I thank you.

There was a time that I longed to understand the importance of everything. Life, death, every, "ism." I longed to understand the benevolence of God. The all powerful, the good that exists in everyone. What is Satan, who is he, why does God allow him to exist? Darwin or Jesus? I'm a Christian, what are you? Born and raised and I still don't understand sometimes why Genesis says, "Let us make man..." Who am I to question? Who are you not to?

Why do you question those things that have founded who you are? Why-

Who am I? Who? What purpose will I serve other than to create and die. Honestly, who will care? Where is the value in creation?

The value is in knowing that what you have done is good.

Good? To live through eyes that judge what I do is good? Eyes that remain closed, seeing only what those eyes have been taught to see. Will I ever understand what makes me who I am? Why can't things be as simple as childhood? Why do we live only to castrate our dreams, to commit suicide, and murder our dreams? The sound does not create the fury, we do. The screams are not in our heads, they are not delusions. We live and breath our obsessions until we have to accept change. Don't we all accept change? I mean, what is the purpose-

Do as you will and live to regret, or live as you dream and live not to regret.

But when does it end?

When you no longer dream.

But I always dream. I dream of walking on cliffs over oceans, falling and floating onto the rocks below. Walking into the sun to see what's there, what other worlds exist. Is there a Heaven? I always dream. From beginning to end, after reading what is born of frustration and joy, I have a sense of faith in everything. I guess. I'm not really sure of what is taking place within me. I'm not sure. Have you ever found that the most comforting thing is that which makes you forget?

Almost a Whisper

Last night she sat and spoke about the old days. I listened and imagined myself there with her. Granny's voice was strong in that motherly way. That voice you heard that made you snap to attention. A voice that could make you shake hands with your biggest enemy. Last night she spoke about the good ol days and I imagined I was there.

"Sweaty, um, um, um. It was hot that year. We was walking a lot anyhow and we found that the longer we walked the closer we got to being where we wanted to be. I mean that in every sense, we got closer. Baby Bruh, always complaining about his feet, was tired, but we didn't care about his feet. We was walkin to freedom. *Precious Lawd take my hand, lead me on*

Hand in hand. A chain link fence of Black folks walking and praising the Lawd. It could have easily been broken up, but for some reason the White folks had just shrugged they shoulders and let us march. I did hear a couple of them, but you could barely make out what they was saying. It was almost a whisper, 'Aww the hell with it, let the niggers march. Thangs been bad enough on em. Hell they deserve one day of peace.' One day of peace. I couldn't believe that they didn't attack us. They jus watched."

I sat and listened to granny and wondered what her purpose was. Why she had decided to sit us all down and talk to us about that day. Usually me and Rene would have to beg her to tell us about that day, and she still wouldn't. Our parents always said that Granny was a part of one of the biggest days in our towns history. But Granny never talked about it. She spoke about every thing else, except that day. We had heard the story from everyone else. But it wasn't until Rene and I sat with Granny and watched that special about all of them marches that she decided to talk to us about that day.

"Yep, show did, jus watched. I thought I was dreamin. I always knew there was some good White folks but it just didn't matter. The rest of em was so bad that every time a seen one White and figured hell, I done seen em all. And then, yaw'll listening? This long White lady in a shiny white dress, with one of them black purses that reflected the sun and sparkled, moved in front of me and broke the line. We all stopped and watched this lady. People in the back was wonderin what was going on. She pushed her purse up onto her arm and grabbed my hand. She also grabbed Rev. Paul's hand and she began to sing. We jus stood there. Then it happened another White person joined in and then another. Until many of them that was watchin and whisperin joined in. Aww glory we shouted and we continued to march. Yes indeed that was somethin. Us Blacks and Whites marched together that day. We talked and marched and the chain fence had grown and we didn't mind at all. Now don't get me wrong all of em didn't join, there was still a couple of em on the side of the street. Watching. I could make out what some of em was sayin, but it didn't matter they words was jus a whisper to the sounds we made that day."

****

I'm afraid sometimes to write things that aren't commercial. But I am also afraid of doing nothing. I want so badly for good things to happen that I sometimes leave myself out there to be, I guess, crucified. Maybe an attempt at writing about the good things should be made, because everything and everyone can't be all bad, can they? And if we decide to find good then I guess the easiest place to start is by looking within and returning to our beginnings.

Sunday Morning when Mahalia Sings

Within this room of flowers and linen
through windows, pushed open, aromas drift.
Pale posters stapled on yellow walls blend,
As soft sounds of gospel, like spirits, lift.

Mom's voice repeats phrases between the riffs.
My senses peak. Smells of breakfast, echoes
from songs, and cool breezes cause me to shift.
I rise and smile, seeing this scene I know.

It hasn't changed, over the years I've grown.
Childhood reflections don't wane as you age,
this day reads like a familiar poem.
Going home, like turning to the page
of a book that you cherish and hold fast,
is that feeling when Mahalia is played.

Now you understand.

Heal The Breach

There is always something that can take the mind to a warm place that pacifies. There are people in our lives who make us recall simpler times. A parent arriving home at ten o'clock at night. Her long days filled with working and demands are not enough to make her forget that you need to be kissed on the forehead. Not enough to make her forget to tuck in your sister, even after the two of you have fought and damn near destroyed the house. Mother can still love you the same.

There is always something. Songs that drift through the air and make us say, "Damn, that's my jam. Aww hell yeah, turn that up." Songs that make us do The Smurf. A lyric, maybe a Gap Band song that we swear we know, that we would fight over to prove that we were right about the words, "Early in the morning, got to find me another, or was it, got to find another lover?"

We never could understand James Brown, but it didn't matter.

There was that ghetto jam that folks in the neighborhood would play over and over, "Money, got to get my hands on some."

There is always that special era that you can recall simply by catching a glimpse of a girl's hair. Class of 89, my girl had a mushroom hair cut.

Seeing a pair of tight ass parachute pants with about thirty zippers on 'em. Maybe that's what this life is all about, dreaming. The dream should be the backdrop, a feeling, a connection. For me, regardless of what happens in this world I can always escape.

Do you really want to escape?

Not really. I love my world, but I love what
we were. Together. Undivided, "Say it loud." You
know? I love today and yesterday, the distant music of
Mingus and Hampton. The one hundred and twenty
eight beats per minute of Public Enemy and KRS-
ONE but,

Despite the incessant boom of ten inch woofers

that drive the music of my era,

I continue to stride into this place where Bird

makes my soul come alive.

Smoke, drifts, and lingers, creating music

on sheets of thin air.

Filters connected to ashtrays also dangle

from quiet lips. Finger snaps propel the moment

as instruments carry the mood to this place,

in this building, in this room, to my booth.

I admire the combination of lyrics and stacked notes.

The sounds of be bop's hi de ho's,

tie into the brassy vocals of Hip Hop,

creating connections when the bass drops.

Chords commence over timeless patterns,

rising melodies, which pace saxophone solos,

that float so low, the sound becomes a Hummm,

before the voice drops in.

The pitch varies in sync with mechanical percussions,

and fuse; Coltrane and Guru, Branford and Buckshot,

two American flavors, the only original flavors,

both labors of love.

There is love for this sound, as I get down

to midnight sessions at the Five Spot;

mixed with vocals labeled, Hot, Phat and Fly.

Some flew on the wings of vices,

which gave license to others to manipulate,

and debate the faults of the righteous.

But I still continue to dig the rhythm of those familiar whispers.

The rhythm, rhyme and repetition, resounds

radically, and rolls around on the wings

of spirits of the past, and the present.

I listen to the horns finding the notes,

that link spirits with the physical.

Pursed, their lips push air through valves that open;

and close in response to fingers that fire

shots of controlled harmony.

I find pleasure in repeating this process of making

the connection.

Can you compare the sound of jazz music?

The earnest strain from fingers closing valves,

tapping symbols softly to create highs,

black and white keys vibrating strings produce

sounds, melodic waterdrops on windows.

Forgotten music from untarnished brass.

An undiscovered sound comes from within.

Heavy baritones hypnotize with chants,

"A Love Supreme, A Love Supreme," a love.

I appreciate all that we have done, regardless of
the hype. We can bring it all together, right?

When Old Men Dance

"I'm too old for that."

"Too old? Pop you're only twenty-nine years older than me."

"And you're twenty -five now right?"

"Yeah but -"

"But nothin. Look son, I just don't do that kind of stuff. I mean when we used to dance-"

"Yaw'll didn't have any feeling. Just in one place shaking your hips side to side. Slow dancing with your hands on each others shoulders. And now all you do is that old man dance where you move your hands and point like you really doing something."

"Now listen, when we danced we moved to the music, in rhythm cause the music meant something. Yaw'll don't do nothin but grind on each other. To some lil boy grabbin his crotch."

"We don't all dance like that. Some of us have a little class."

"Boy shut it and go fix me a glass of lemonade."

"All right pops." Pops lay back on the couch and pushed the red button on the remote.

"Dammit son. What the hell is this noise? Bump, bump, bumpity thump. You on point Tip. What the heck is on point tip? This just ain't music son."

"That's Tribe Pops. They're a real positive hip hop crew. Just listen to the words. It's the clean version."

"Thank you son. What's that you say? The clean version. Why you need two versions of the same song? I mean yaw'll kids, I don't know."

"I guess that's a good question dad. Real good question. Let's go out to the porch."

"Son, let me tell you a story bout real music and dancing."

"A real story huh? Go head Pops tell me the real story."

"Your mother, was a real slick dancer. We was at a block party back in sixty-eight and this new group from Motown, you may have heard of them."

"Who were they -"

"Don't interrupt me, they was the Temptations. A real singing group, nothin like these begging, shouting, yelling singers yaw'll got now."

"Hold on pop, we got Boyz 2 Men. They pretty good, you even said it yourself."

"All right yaw'll got one group."

"Take Six, Pops, you said you liked them too."

"All right, let me finish boy. Like I was saying, your mom heard the intro and she stood up and shimmied over to me-"

"Shimmied Pop? Shimmying sounds real close to shaking and grinding."

"Be quiet now. Your mama grabbed me by the hand and we danced through the next ten records. Boy we was jukin."

"You know what Pop? That sounds like a story you could have told today. I mean we still do that kind of thing. The music has changed a lot, but we still do some of those thangs yaw'll did."

"Well, maybe you did. Son go turn the radio back on."

"Why? You gonna listen to it for a change?"

"Yeah, and I want you to show me one of them new dances. I like that butterfly dance. I wanna teach your mama that one."

"You crazy Pops. I love you."

"I love you too son."

****

The last thirty years?

We changed but there are still those moments, new moments. Every ending means that there will be a new beginning. To dwell on the past, is to repeat it. To remain in sadness can blind you to the happiness that awaits everyone. I have moved on and I can feel it.

This is the process. I can understand the highs and lows. The blocks, the late night call from the oracle. Forcing you to slide to the keyboard in darkness and listen to the chime as your computer welcomes you. This is the process. Tears shed over past loves, tears shed over confusion and hate. Smiles given to someone new. A friend who tells you that it's okay to call a Black man brother and mean it. This is the process. Sitting and wondering how the story will end, deciding if the plot is understandable and genuine enough for someone to give a damn about. How can I pretend to be sad, you can see it in the words. I somewhat question myself for moving on ...

This is the process. An increase in tempo, the voice changes and manipulates you. Can you feel it? Maybe for things to take the correct form one has to believe in what they are doing. You have to serve a purpose right? I can feel my heart pound the closer I come to true love, (and I hate that word :-) But I can't avoid it. She has definitely got me believing in myself again. This woman who has moved me from the darkness, away from my block. The time we share is so inspiring. Initial questions of past relationships that were tossed to the side. Dark the first few months, and then all the shades over the windows are opened allowing the truth to enter. Through it all I have found that she is what I've been searching for. Even when I failed to believe in her she was what I longed for. The seeming repetition in tapping and waiting for the structure to form the plot, is not really repetition if the words change during each hour spent with her. I think, I finally realize why she has come back to me. Different and still the same in her beauty and knowledge. I will never leave her, this is who I am.

Late nights are welcome. As long as I have music and dreams, hate and love, I will continue to do the will of the story. On days when I can't see the sun, when things don't seem to be so bright, I will continue. As long as we know that change is okay, we can continue together, as long as we listen.

I think I believes that this time you are serious.

I am.

I now see that writing is more than just something to do. It takes dedication and honesty. Building a foundation that will last, is not easy. But it is worth it when you change a person's perception. Yes it is for us to entertain, but in doing so we can't forget to give our words meaning. We have to understand that a word created for one purpose, can come to serve another. Negative can become positive, sometimes. But I think we should check ourselves in doing this. We should ensure that we aren't making the wrong words into something positive.

This Brother, Charles

"Yeah man I can dig it. Right on, right on." Charles said.

"This ain't the seventies man. What the hell you mean, right on? Niggas was killin each other in the seventies too."

"Yeah, you right man."

"Don't you have something else to say? I mean damn you said that brothers got problems now. What you mean?"

"We got problems. But we used to be man enough to confront our problems. Now we got problems. Listen-"

"Man I swear yaw'll niggas is all the same. Nigga leave and go to college, this nigga thank he the shit now.

"Like I said, we got problems. Brothers used to be able to say that white folks holdin him back, right?"

"Cracker bastards still holdin us back."

"Yeah, you right. I'll get back at you later after you listen to yourself. When you can hear what you're saying then holla at me later, you dig?"

"Go head on and go back to college nigga. You still a nigga."

"Naw brother, you still a nigga."

This brother Charles knew it. But the fellas didn't listen. I heard him. I knew what he was tryin to say but I can't lie, I ain't smart enough to go to school, but I wanna go. But the rest of these niggas 'll front me off and say I'm tryin to be like Charles. Damn man, I know I'm smarter than this neighborhood. I ain't got to stay here, I just ain't got to, but I don't know. Charles don't even kick with us too much no more. He always got homework and shit. Nigga always talking to some bitch about this, that, and the other. I see why the fellas don't like his ass no more. But I still kinda like Charles. Tell the truth, I wish I was like him. Man that nigga Charles is all right. Maybe I should ask him to hook me up. A nigga graduated from high school two years ago and I ain't doing shit but staying at home and working. Maybe I'll call him, hell he said call him. He was right. We got problems, but at least we ain't slaves no more. Them motherfuckers had problems. Them brothers in them old videos and shit had problems. That brother Charles is all right, fuck the fellas. I think I'ma call him.

****

When the does the dream deferred become rerouted and shipped by way of Fed Ex or UPS to us? Or do we go out and get the deferred package instead of waiting on reparations. Who is really holding us back? Who?

There was an old spiritual folks used to sing when they was in the fields. One that everyone used to sing. Folks don't know the words anymore. Folks don't want to sing the same song, they don't realize that a song can be sung thousands of ways as long as everybody has at least memorized the words. Memorized them enough to trust in them. Memorized them enough to maybe hum the tune.

Do you know the words?

I do.

Lawd done let us live jus one mo day,

Lawd done let us live jus one mo day,

And if I dies tomaruh,

Lawd ain't lef me here alone

Lawd ain't lef me here alone

Long as my peoples know dis song

Da Lawd ain't lef me here alone.

What does it mean, this song that we used to sing?

It means what we were.

The ambiguity of such a statement seems rather poetic. But sometimes it may be better to say what you mean without any vagueness. I understand what you are saying. How do you express it now. That was a different time. We didn't die then, like we do know. There was a blame to be placed then, and it was.

There is a blame to place now. Should we? Should we blame?

I have found that a story is told for a reason. Even the greatest story is flawed, but it isn't the writer that decides that his story is flawed.

What?

People make other people into what they desire. A person allows the greater norms to dictate who they are. A race can commit genocide by justifying even the smallest thing.

I see.

I choose not to call you nigga,

that, my brother, isn't my style.

I refuse to call you whitey,

while at work, in your face, I smile.

I don't like to refer to you

as a kike, or tight-fisted Jew;

But if you call me porch monkey,

what do you expect me to do?

Though your eyes may appear smaller,

that still doesn't make your race blind.

Your religion may be Islam,

does that mean I don't trust your kind?

Your features may be different,

your skin may be another hue;

I recall when we were children,

color had no place in our views.

Why is there a negative word for every race? Why do We justify using this word as one of love. I don't know of any word in history, that has been used to verbally destroy a race that has been reconsidered as a word of endearment. How can a justification be made for using that word in any other context than what it has always meant?

Destroy the word, begin to destroy that past.

How do I do that when so many accept it as their own?

Write.

My Mother

Hot. Sweat rolled down my mother's face as she struggled to keep pace with everyone else. Mattie, from over on Fifth Street, and Paula stood beside her. Their arms interlocked. Long, pasty blue dresses on, with white socks flipped over. Patent leather shoes shining, absorbing every ray from the sun. Three shades of beautiful Black. Walking. Woolworth's loomed in the distance. Almost like a mirage wavering. The heat making the sign in front look like smoke drifting from a hot skillet. Mom continued between the two women. Singing. Preparing. The group of thirteen all on key. Her feet slipped inside of her shoe. Her stomach heavy and round, full of life. She walked. Marching. Finally making it to the COLOREDS ONLY entrance of the store, they abided, and made their way in. The dining counter was not exempt from the heat. The large, glass windows barely covered by pale white curtains. Three young White men sat at the end of the long counter, eating. Several old women looked at the group of coloreds.

"Dem NIGGERS ain't sposed to be in here is they?" A white haired old man said loudly. The room was quiet. Shiny, chrome stools placed in front of the counter. The cooks stared. The waitresses continued, working. My mother sat between Paula and Mattie. The men with them gathered around and then sat at the tables. Mom sat with her stomach away from the counter. Blond, the first waitress, whispered in mom's ear, "Read the sign NIGGER." Mom sat arching her back. The weight bothering her. Sweat trickling. The three White boys left their food. Standing,

"No NIGGERS allowed. Can't you coons read?"

The tallest boy walked over and threw his drink at one of the colored boys. Passive,

Mom tried to order. The heavy boy listened and walked towards her. His lips close to her eyes. Hand full of biscuits and butter. Talking, he spat crumbs of wet dough in mom's face. She sat.

"This NIGGER here kinda plump yaw'll."

Paula stood in front of my mother, protective. The heavy boy pushed Paula aside. Mattie grabbed mom's arm and began to leave. Mom stopped Mattie. The others sat. The third boy reached around and poured thick, warm molasses on mom's hair. She stood. Everyone stood and watched. The old women laughed, one of them whispered, "Tar and feather." They laughed.

The syrup ran down mom's dress and pooled on top of a spot on her stomach. Afraid. The heavy boy took his left hand and pulled mom by the hair. She fell. The colored boys picked her up. Sweating. Mom was breathing heavily. The boys carried her as fast as they could. Dying. My older sibling would have been thirty-one today.

"I hate that word," mom always tells me.

A term of endearment now?

Only so much can be said about our choice of words. What we create everyday. Never the same sentence, always a new paragraph. I still can't watch the videos, but I don't need to. One was enough to firmly graft its tattoo onto my soul. This, these words, are a part of who I am. The chains, whips, songs, the freedom, I am all of these things and I am proud. What makes me truly happy is knowing that what I do means something, no matter what becomes of these words that fill the screen. I am no longer afraid.

And what was it that you were afraid of? What is it that you have become?

A writer.

Short Stories

Begin

No matter what happens a blooming flower, a newborn baby, galloping horses on open land, will all remain beautiful. This is to say one thing, moving beyond the norm is never desired by anyone. Really, it isn't. Acceptance, NOW, NAACP,... Irrelevant. You are who you are and I am who you think I am. Stories randomly tossed about are created not for the sake of art, but out of an existence of opportunity. Skin is the moderator. In silence, fear grows and self righteousness is the factor which manipulates the order of the day. What was it Eddie Murphy said, 'Give a Nigger a rope and a Nigger wanna be a cowboy.' Nah that doesn't fit. I know what summed it up best. *The Five Heartbeats* , in the one scene before Eddie Kane prepares to go on tour with the group and the dad is waiting outside, what is it he says, 'You ain't shit. You ain't never gon be shit, just like me.' Then again I guess that's not it either. I think maybe the statement, 'I brought you into this world and I can take you out,' fits better. But then that leaves the question of what is really being addressed here and how long can I hide what my real point is. Ice Cube, "I'm that Nigga you love to hate." Jay Z, "Nigga what, Nigga who?" Mos Def, "Who be riding up in the high rise elevator other neighbors be praying he ain't they new neighbor? Mr. Nigga, Nigga, Nigga." Jeru the Damaja, "Niggas are in state of helplessness, nothingness." Your subconscious, "What is this Nigga doing?"

'Nothing.'

In e whey, creative license: I killed two motherfuckers last week. Smoked two joints laced with some kind of fucked up dust and jumped them motherfuckers from behind a garbage can. I took they shit and said fuck it. I got high and went back out in the street. Funny shit was, while I was killing one of em the other motherfucker just stood there looking. I was on some serious shit though. It had me thinking, "I'm OJ, I'm fucking OJ." As I eased the fucking blade across throats and eyes. I didn't give a flying shit that these was somebodies' moms and dads. I needed the money. I needed the high, both of them.

Creative License: I got fucking drunk last week dude. I went out and got smashed you know? Regardless of other people I was chilling and hanging with my buds, doing stupid shit you know? Okay here it is, here it is. About two thirty a.m. I was gunning the fucking engine on the highway just fucking around, I was drinking, that shit is fun ain't it? You drink so don't front, but this shit was crazy. I jumped in the car and kept pulling it out of gear on the expressway going like eighty. I mean I was having fun drinking not five minutes earlier you know? Anyways this guy was pulling onto the highway from the Coca Cola plant I guess. And I had to swerve but the car wasn't in gear so I tipped the front of his car. I slapped my car into gear and kept going. He was fucking okay, I'm sure. I was drinking isn't that cool though. I know damn well nothing happened. Shit no responsibility, is no responsibility and I didn't stop so I don't have any responsibility. Besides I'm sure he's okay. It's funny right?

Creative License: I don't know how much ass I got in the last year or so. But I found out last week I had Herpes and that shit is fucked up. I'm sure some bitch gave it to me.

Mr. Nigga... Nigga, Nigga. That's what it's about huh. Your subconscious, "The fuck is he trying to prove?"

"Nothing."

I read *The Colored Museum* a while back and damn near died laughing. You know what that is right? *Fences*? Okay plays don't do it for everybody. I read *The Vulture*... No. *Small Talk at 125 and Lennox*? No? That shit is important to me though, you had to read them didn't you? Alright damn, submission, figure four leg lock and I can't reach the ropes. I read *The Sound and the Fury* a while back and man was it good. The best shit I ever read. Better than Bigger, not Biggie, better than Stamp Paid, any Black shit I ever read. It had to be though didn't it?

Thirteen, twelve, eleven, how much longer will your interest be held. Probably not long. I don't have anymore alcohol in me. That sucks. Funny huh? I guess. Okay story time:

In dull gray skin his blood coursed and flowed. Tired. Foster had given all of his energy to the mine and there, Billy had died and Tony. Recently, he found out that his lungs were Black as well. Crusted, coated with the shit and there was nothing that could be done except slow death. His insurance coverage was more for his son, daughter and wife than him. So he kept working. He didn't tell no one. Not a single soul... but Frankie knew. He had watched the coughing, the nosebleeds with Foster. When both Tony and Billy took ill he spoke to Foster about it. It took them to die in the fucking pit to stop showing up. But Foster still saw them, everyday. Dead whiteys told no lies. They spoke to him, airy words,

"You next Nigga, yep sho is. You next and you ain't been here half as long as we was."

"Then why?"

"Cause hell you wadn't spose to be here in the first place."

"Both of yaw'll can go to hell."

"We will. We just waiting on you darkie. Just waiting on you."

That's it for that story. I just wanted to see if I could do something semi-dramatic. Like I was saying I was reading this book/ play, *The Colored Museum* and fuck it if you've never heard of it. You don't have to sit and read Black shit right? If you wanted to do that you would take Black Studies classes. There aren't any Black Classics. Okay, okay, I'm lying but right on, write on.

Blunts and Hip Hop go together like Farts and Mouths. Exactly. You want that shit to fit though. I am. I am Black. I am Black in. I am Blackened Salmon. Ha Ha. Okay. I am a Black writer. To you I am music, sports, Eddie Murphy, and nothing else. Don't say that's not true, it is. I have no further depth to me than the distance from your eyes to my skin. That shit disturbs me. But does it hinder, no. I am not a Nigger, Nigga. My mother doesn't like that word and neither do I. But I can hear you thinking it right now. Don't lie. Fuck you too. That's better isn't it. Get it out. All that doubt about who I am, what I do, and then we can get on with what's important White stories full of mystery, intrigue, historical literary references, you know the important stuff. I can't write that shit. But of course you say I can. Come on now, you know better. Black is Black and it represents Black. I know you are saying, "You are limiting your self." That's mighty whitey of you. Privilege of Anonymity. 'I want to be White,' said the little girl with nappy hair and big lips. "Barbie's beautiful. The Black Barbie's are fake looking."

The beginning is set at a university on the west coast. The Golden State, the southern most tip before you reach the Natives. A professor gives an assignment in a program where there are only maybe two Black men. The class room is cold. He sits alone in the room and watches face after face entering hoping for familiarity. There isn't any, even in the faces he likes. He sits in the corner and shucks and jives. Call him Mr. Bojangles, happy to dance for you. No matter what I do in your subconscious I am basketball, Hip Hop and Redd Foxx. That shit bothers me. But here is where the story begins. Where the end begins. I will kill you all before the end and resurrect you in the name of Nat Turner, carry you back on the Black Star Line. I got a rhyme for you. I don't know the shit you know, It'll take me a lifetime to catch up. Privileged. That shit pisses me off, but at least you know the truth now. So we can begin. May I have this dance, my razor is under my tongue, sharp and warm. Yes, lettuce dance.

"Free Jass"

That music be alright to me in the loudest moments and quietest times. Not no noise, white noise, interfering with them sounds bleating and thumping. I can hear that movement in the beginning riff and then it all let loose, cause ain't no sound like when music be free, ain't no sound like when music be free. Yessir that music be alright to me. I figure if I was born in another place at another time, say New York City early fifties, then things work out for me jus fine. I coulda walked on over to the artsy part of town to get on down with cats like Ornette and listen to Kerouac. I figure White boys got soul too, sometimes. Even if I couldn't go to any other place to see or here Coleman, I coulda heard them when they first got it going. Three Brothers and a White cat, who could slap that bass silly. I mean, to be standing there in the Five Spot, packed in with funky, wet Whiteys and heavy jazz Blacks watching that painting come to life. Oh man, to see cigarette smoke jumping up to outline faces with dark shades, and glasses clinking together to toast birthdays or new pieces... man.

I got this groove in my head that I know I coulda rapped on a table in there and fit right in. Rap a ta tat tat, crack a ta tat tat, be dum a dump tap a ta tat, clack we dee be de dah. Rap a ta tat tat. I mean this rhythm I got is catchy and it feels good. It ain't some modal piece by Miles that everybody comfortable with, not that that's a bad thing. I just figure on being one of the few young cats who now the difference in art and using controlled substances. Okay maybe Coltrane can share the plate but I'm not reaching for God right now, well not reaching for him in my pleasure. And I do take some pleasure in discovering a new sound after listening to the same song for the umpteenth time. If women can buy songbirds and think that's jazz, then I can damn sure spend my free time admiring the truth.

And maybe that doesn't have anything to do with anything but at least I can claim this sound as my mantra in a way. My lady she didn't dig it much and think it sounded weird. She always ask me if I ever thought it sounded out of tune. It ain't that I ain't never thought that, but when you become so in tune with the music, you forget that the sounds are far removed from dead center.

It wasn't a sound that didn't fit in even when I first heard it and I don't really care much what other folks think and say towards my music. I listen to it and hear it. It's common sense. If you can play, then play. Ain't that the way life is?

My lady, she dug the heavy bass of some booty shaking song, but what was tripped to me was how some of the booty shaking songs was Gospel, but I didn't love her no less for this discrepancy. She didn't love me no less. I guess we was built that way. We was easy to keep in love. Not too many fights and arguments, to build no shallow false love on, like most folks do. We got through to each other. We something supersonic. Something felt, not seen or heard. We was on this transmission that nobody else could hear. It wasn't the answering questions, before the question was asked or the constant jokes, but it was this fear we had that made us how we were. I still got that fear. Holding on to it for some reason or another.

Black men ain't supposed to cry.

"She love me, she love me not."

"Love you not."

"Don't play."

"Not playing with you, just-"

"Don't play."

"Watcha gonna do? Huh? You gonna force me to listen to that bad music. What is it, Acid Jazz?"

"Why is it that my music is bad? It's intellectual."

"So you saying my paper on the wall ain't equal to yours? I'm not an intellectual?"

"Some folks ain't got the mental-"

"Watch it."

Rolling in bed for hours on Saturday morning. No work to do. Just love to share and time. We didn't talk about much to most folks and didn't feel there was much sharing needed to be done, except with each other. We always had playing time and when it did get serious we was so casual and frequent with discussions that it wasn't nothing we couldn't tackle. An argument lasted a day at the most. If tossing the word love around takes the power out of the phrase, "I love you," then she was the only woman that wasn't bothered much by that and it was beautiful.

But she got the notion to dip into my life too far. I hid myself from her and that hiding saved her, and me. I never got to see her look at me when I was there, in that place, in that fog. But I could hear so well when I was there. Hear it all. The voice spoke and the baby crying, the deep voice telling me it was alright, but that shit was all gone now and wasn't no way to get it back and be right. It ain't no sunshine cause she's gone and now all I got is this music that nobody else get cept for old folks.

It's taking me a whole lifetime to get over her, but folks say it should take Black folks forty years to get right. My baby knew me, she knew, and felt like me writing and listening shoulda been separate. I didn't owe nobody specially not Ornette.

"Ain't no way he your muse. I mean the man can barely get a gig nowadays. The way I see it, if he your muse then you a living contradiction."

"How so?"

"Ain't it called Free?"

"It is and it is."

"But you ain't. You can't even share your thoughts on paper without addressing us. Black folks ain't with you and white folks don't give a damn about what you writing."

"Giving a damn ain't what it's for, you got it all confused."

"Confused I am, but for some reason, I'm still here. I can't figure it out. It's like you got roots on me. I always thought you was creole and all. Besides, only a man from New Orleans can be so damn confused."

"You lucky I like you."

"You lucky I love you."

"You love my writing?"

"Do I have to?"

"Guess not."

"Yeah."

"Yeah what?"

"Yeah to all your answers. Don't be trapped in all that. One day you gonna wake up and have to discover what free really mean."

"Until that time I'm free."

"Ain't no freedom in creating with a slant for folks who don't care, whether you getting paid for it or not."

It ain't no freedom in it. My losses, all this around me, the cars, house, all this seem distant from me now. Her hair still tickle my nose when I sleep, and every day seem like the last track I can find when I'm shooting this free.

Her gone nah and this here music got me feeling in darker hues, and blues is what I'm hearing when I come down writing for us, still making me confused. I'm sorry love.

I Found It Hidden

It interrupted what had been a steady stream of creativity. It had interrupted my creative will and I allowed it. There was a billboard above her head. I saw it through my window. I failed to put it all on paper at the time, but a vivid memory is often as good as a new memory. There was dust and old pieces of newspaper gathered at the base of the sign. The idea of old news gathering beneath a billboard offering low long distance rates intrigued me. I sat at my keyboard typing away trying to ignore the water forming on my brow. My armpits, moist with clumps of deodorant no longer hiding the smell, became a distinct motivation for an odd story of a young man held in the hole of a prison.

Sitting in a concrete cell with dusty floors, large cockroaches scraping wings along the floor and this boy sitting in his own shit. A rather long cliche of what being trapped is like, was what this story could become.

Yet the newspapers under the billboard, with the huge fluorescent light humming, continued to hold me captive.

Light entered the boy's cell, broken into four sections by small poles in an iron door. A grainy image of shadows beneath his door faded into the darkness of his cell.

Who was he? The papers outside ruffled and slid over to the brick wall behind the tall pole holding the sign. Paint chipping off of the pole in blue flakes that caught the rough material of her dress. Her heavy legs covered, with old black stockings like thick tree stumps covered in oil, seemed rooted to that spot. Her hair fluffed in a blonde bun sat like a hat on top of thick course hair. The heel of her shoe plunged through a copy of the Tribune into a picture of some headline story.

Footsteps passing by the cell caused him to stand and listen for keys jingling outside of his door. He listened to the footsteps continue down the hall.

Her lipstick was red like a stoplight, shiny red. I saw the car pull up to the corner. Her dress, grabbing every lump of flesh within, pushed her breasts out. But it was dark like inside the boy's cell.

I think his name is Rell. He could hear the guards outside laughing. His name mentioned twice in the past few minutes, or hours maybe.

I could see this guy getting out of the car, a long blade in his hands, but that was all I saw.

Rell's cell door opened and Mitchell, the White guard walked in with a hose. The water beat Rell's arms and legs as he moved into the corner, in a ball. His skin burned, the pain like small fastballs hitting him at ninety-five miles an hour. His eyes still bright because at least he would be leaving, escaping this block.

Underneath the sign small splatters covered the wall and the newspapers, but the woman was gone, the car, the woman, both like ghosts. I'm sure I imagined it all. Writing it down now has moved me past it. It had interrupted a creative surge which hadn't been with me since the day I saw her underneath that billboard. The fluorescent light cut off at five-thirty that morning and the splatter looked like busted packets of ketchup on the wall. It probably was ketchup there was a burger bag mixed in with the newspapers that remained stuck to the pole.

Mitchell moved Rell back into general population and apologized for how he was treated. A sincere apology. It had been three and a half years since he had been outside of the prison and it felt odd. His mother picked him up outside the jail and took him home. Rell closed the passenger door and fell back into his seat. The sun gleamed through the glass into his eyes. He blinked and held them shut for a moment, noticing the red light through his skin. His mother asked him questions which he didn't hear. He had drifted back to the actions of the past few days. Samson this heavyset brother, who kept his hair cut in this jarhead fashion, saw fit to place him in the hole for his last four days inside. It was Samson's twisted tradition for many of the Black inmates who were close to being released.

"You boys wanna act like niggers, Ima give you a reason to hate this here place. Consider this *yo ntroducshun to the plantation nigger.* Better yet, this here is da *Amistad.*"

Rell listened as he pushed him into the cell. Wind rushed out as the door opened. His naked skin tingled from the cold, musty air. His eyes looked beyond his thick eyebrows at Samson. He felt as if he could have killed the bastard. How many times had Samson done this. Mitchell didn't like it, he knew that the it was some kind of reflection on Samson's childhood.

"Ay man don't you git tired of doing that kinda stuff? I mean I could see if you was one of these biggots in here. Hell they don't even-"

"Fuck off Mitch, let me handle this. These are my people, I'm just tryin to make sho they don't never wanna comeback. I'm-"

"You think they wanna be here? Man what the fuck is your trip. I ain't got no part in this shit this time Sam."

Rell looked at Samson and decided then that he really understood what hate was. He knew he didn't want to be there, not on some bullshit car theft charge. Twenty-one was still young enough to be something. What was this brothers trip he thought? Had he had his ass kicked by brothers when he was young, maybe abandoned by his folks, or some sister fucked him over. Rell had to question him but at what cost would his answers come.

"Say bruh why you do this kind of thing?"

Samson punched Rell in his stomach with his baton and spat on him.

"Don't fucking ask me shit *boy*."

"I was just," the stick caught Rell beneath his left rib. His muscular frame dropped to the floor, dust rose into the air.

"I said don't talk."

"Sam, what the fuck dude?" Mitchell ran in and grabbed him by the arm. "I got this man, you need to go and cool out."

"Yeah you right. Fucking nigga wanna ask me questions and shit. Smart ass." Samson walked out adjusting his shirt with a smile on his face.

"Rell, you only got a few days left man you know the routine."

"I just wanted to know."

"What?"

"Why he don't like his own folks man. I mean damn you seem to care."

"It's just my job to act like I care. I could give a fuck about you, you're in here for a reason. Ain't no saints in jail."

"None?"

"Maybe one or two," Micthell smiled and sat on the floor beside Rell.

"Damn Rell why didn't you play football or some shit?"

"All Black men have to play football or basketball?"

"I didn't say that-"

"Just fucking with you Mitchell. Thought about it man, I still can. Maybe in junior college."

"Samson."

"Fuck Samson."

"He was abused man. I read his files. Dude been transferred from like three different correctional facilities."

"Abused, so that means that he gets to fuck up every brother he meets now?"

"Look here, you got three days left. Just let this shit ride out easily, don't ruffle any feathers."

"Thanks Mitchell."

"Yeah."

As the sun came up over the billboard I felt a sense of relief. I closed my blinds walked into my bedroom and attempted to let my dreams take me away from the stories, both real and made-up. Sleep overtook me quickly until Rell's mother spoke. I shot towards the computer and shook the mouse.

"Baby what is you going to do wit yoself? Ms. Betty an me was talkin bout you. You gotta do sumthin or you gon end up back in there."

Rell scratched his forehead and looked back out towards the street. The trees shot by in a blur. He rolled down the window and let the warm, moist air fill the car.

"I ain't going back mom. I can't go back." He said looking out the window.

"Well, we figured that you could work at Johnny's biness. Helping cut grass over yonder in Whitehaven. Dem rich folks payin him purty good."

"Cut grass?"

"Nah look here ain't nuttin much wrong wit cuttin grass. It's a job, a payin job."

"Momma I was thinking maybe I should go to college. I'm gon have to go if I want to get anywhere in life."

"Well right nah you jus needs to be workin. You ain't gon be gettin back in dem streets runnin wild."

Rell rolled the window up and let the heat fill the car. The air condition didn't seem to be blowing hard enough to cool him down. The sweat traced the large bones in his cheeks following a path down to his chin, dropping on to his shirt lapel. Cuttin grass wouldn't be so bad for a while. Besides it was early in summer and he had another month before he would have to start trying to get in school. He sat back in the seat and listened to his mother speak about how the neighborhood had changed since he was gone.

"Baby when you leff them other boys didn't do nuthin. Not nuthin. Hangin round smoking an sellin dem drugs. All night in da streets. Mmmm Hmmm, that's right. Reverend Fisher don had rally after rally to git dem off da streets, but he can't do much. Dem boys ain't scared of him no mo. Just last week they broke in the church an stole all last weeks offerins."

Rell sat up in his seat.

"Mom, they stole the offerings? Who was it Eddie and them?"

"Well, baby Eddie don got killed in a shootin about a week ago."

"Why didn't you tell me that mom?"

"Cause you didn't need to know, I ain't lettin you git in with dem boys. I ain't lettin it happen. You gon git a lit rest an then you goin out to Whitehaven wit Johnny."

The car coasted down the street turning onto Danny Thomas, into Hurt Village.

"Man, the projects ain't changed at all," Rell said looking at the rows of brick buildings lining the street.

"Da Rev. said dat's why they call dem projeks."

"What mom?"

"Dey is projeks, cause they a work in progress. A neverendin job fuh the govment to keep us Black folk wantin nuttin and knowin nuttin. Da projeks."

His eyes looked at the apartments. The long, black bars covering the windows. The light breaking into lines shining through.

"He right mom."

As she pulled into her parking space she could see several boys with beer and cigarettes walking towards the car. One of them had a poster with 'Welcome Home Rock'. Rell looked at them and then at the bars on the windows of the apartments once more. Ms. Jenkins climbed out the car and waved the boys off.

"Gon nah he tired. He don't need you boys messin wit him."

"What's up nigga," yelled Baby Tony, Frank and Cutty. Wiz stood in the back eyeing Rell, sizing him up.

"Welcome back home man, shit it's good to see you." Cutty said, giving Rell a pound with his fist.

"What's the deal Rock, you gon kick it man?" said Frank.

Rell looked at the group and then at his mom standing in front of the house with her purse in her hand.

"Ay, I'll holla at yaw'll later, I'm real tired. Later, thanks for the welcome."

Wiz walked up behind the group slowly.

"Let's go, fuck that nigga. He think he better than us cause he been to jail and shit. Cause he got bigger and shit."

"Wiz why you trippin. That's Rock man," said Baby Tony.

"And I'm the motherfucking Wizard. I put this shit together after he left. Remember that."

Rell looked out the window and listened in on what was being said.

"Baby you gon have to be careful. Dem boys ain't like dey use to be."

"I know mom. I know."

Rell looked around the house and realized that the light came into the room unhindered. Full and steady, the sun filled the room as small dust particles landed on the couch.

"You got a new TV?"

"Dat's yo welcome home gift. Baby, I wants you to go on out yonder to Whitehaven, cause your momma worried."

"I'll be okay mom."

After two weeks of working with Johnny, Rell began to call for information about going to community college. The packets were bulky. The mailman had to bring the envelopes to the door. All the information was like French to Rell as he tried to make sense of it all. He carried the packet with him to work. Johnny had finished his landscaping degree at Lane, before he started his business. While they sat on the porch at the Overbrook Estate, about an acre of land with a sprawling garden, Johnny talked to him about the packet.

"How you holding up today?"

"I'm cool."

"It's hot as hell huh? Bet you can cook an egg on the street today."

"Yeah."

"So you thinking about going to college? I went to Lane."

"For real?"

"Yep sure did. Gave me a damn good start."

"Johnny, do they let people in that have records."

"Yeah, I got Marvin Gaye and an Earth, Wind and Fire album that I played on campus all the time."

"Forget it man."

"Calm down Rell, I'm just foolin with you. You can go to school with a record. As a matter of fact they have counselors that work specifically with ex cons."

"Don't call me an ex con. I got a record, cons kill people and shit, I ain't no fuckin ex con."

Johnny stood holding his hands up, trying to calm Rell. The old man came out on the porch, his stringy, silver hair standing on his head.

"Lookey here, I pay you *boys* to keep my grass, not to raise Cain on my porch."

"Sorry about that sir, we gettin right back to it. Just taking a break."

"Allright, just quiet down or I'll send you on your way without paying you."

Rell looked at the way Johnny was responding to the old man. All submissive and apologetic.

"Why did you act like that with him?"

"Like what?"

"Like an Uncle Tom." Johnny walked off the porch and sat on his lawnmower. Rell followed him.

"This ain't the fifties man."

"Rell, shut up," Johnny said softly. "Shut up and listen. People are set in their ways sometimes. When you have to make a living, you have to put up with some things. Mr. Overbrook pays well and refers. I make a lot of money off of him."

"But at what cost? He treating you like a field nigger."

"Yeah, but a field nigger didn't make sixty thousand a year."

"I don't know Johnny, it ain't right for a man to do things to you cause of his complex."

"You're a smart boy Rell, but this is America-"

"Don't give me that shit about America. We make our own decisions now. I stole them cars and shit. Nobody forced me to do it."

"Calm down Rell, all I'm saying is that to make it you have to take a little stuff off of people and ain't nothing wrong with that."

"I guess."

"Let's get back to work. I'll help you with that application and stuff when we finish."

"I just don't like the way he called us *boys*."

"Let it rest."

On the way back to Rell's house, Johnny talked about how hard college was.

"Johnny I ain't proud of it, but I stole cars. A car thief can't be stupid."

"Bull."

"Allright some of them can, but I'm not stupid. I could've done okay in school. Just didn't want to."

"That's stupid."

"I know."

"Why you always saying you know? Obviously you don't. Rell you're gonna have to start listening and then reacting."

"I don't get it."

"The downfall of man is the way we react. Check this out-"

"I get it, if you listen you can prepare."

"Right."

"Told you I wasn't stupid."

"Never said that you was."

Johnny pulled into the parking lot beside Mama Softstone's car. Franky walked over slapped Rell's hand and asked him if he was going to kick it with the fellas.

"Yo Rock, the fellas said you changed dawg. I don't think so, but on the real if you did, you betta watch your back nigga." Franky laughed and ran towards the rest of the group.

"Watch your back huh?"

"Yeah Johnny I heard that kind of stuff inside. It didn't bother me then and I ain't gon let it bother me now."

"Maybe you should."

"I do but if I let it mess with my head I lose control, and the worst thing a brother can do is lose his head."

"Damn jail made you into a thinker. That's dangerous."

"I know, but I had to think or I woulda got killed man. Too much to live for."

"That's right, let's get inside. I bet your mom has got something good to eat."

"Yeah I know."

"You always know. We'll see if you know how to fill out those financial aid papers."

The living room smelled of roses from a large basket of potpourri placed on the table by the door.

The fan was in the window pushing the air around just enough to keep the house cool. Rell could hear his Mom on the phone.

"Yes suh, yes suh, I'll be there in da mornin. I'll take care of it then. Allright suh yaw'll have a good day."

"Mom that hotel will fall apart if you leave."

"Naw it won't baby, dem White folks just don't like doin da dirty stuff. Dey is always picky bout doin everthang. I figure if I do it then I always got a place to work."

"Hmph," Rell said listening to words that rang in his head.

"Let's get started with this package Rell. The sooner we sift through all this stuff the sooner we finish."

"Mom is there some food in the kitchen?"

"Nah baby, your momma too tired to cook today. Go head an order you some pizza, I got some good tips today."

"Rell how old is your mom?"

"I guess she about fifty-four now. When I went in she was like fifty-one."

"Okay, first you have to fill out this here application for the school." Rell began writing as his mom poured them two glasses of lemonade. before she sat down and put her feet up on the stool in front of her chair.

"Nah I know college good for him, but how he gon work and make good grades?"

"He can get financial aid."

"Financing aid? Where that money come from? Is it the school?"

"Kind of, it's from the government it-"

"I don't want my son on no govment help. I ain't nevuh been on no welfare an I ain't gon start my son on no welfare. The Reverend said dat the system is set up to keep us folks dependent on dem. I don't want no part of it."

"Hold on nah, keep writing Rell. Some of the money is free if he qualifies which I think he will."

"Free? Ain't nuthin free you know that."

"He gon have to keep his grades up to get the assistance. Please just trust me I wouldn't do anything to hurt Rell."

Outside the door they heard two voices arguing about some,

"Look homie that motherfucker owe us both some ends and I ain't gon let him get away with that. How would that make me look?"

"Wiz, man if Frank had your stuff man he wouldn't hold out. I'm tellin-"

"You tellin?" Wiz grabbed Cutty by the throat and pushed him into the door. Rell jumped up.

"Ay get that shit off my doorstep."

"Your doorstep? Yo this shit ain't been yours in a long time. I got this now partna. You need to get your ass back in the house and let me handle my business."

Rell opened the screendoor and stepped off of the porch.

"Look I ain't got no beef with you. I don't want no part of this drug shit, it's all yours-"

"I know that. You damn right it's all mine."

"I'm just saying get this stuff off my doorstep. That's all."

Ms. Softstone walked out and Johnny followed. They attempted to get Rell to go back in the house.

"Yeah take his bitch ass back in the house. Before I eff him up Ms. Stone."

"Boy you ain't got no respect,"Johnny said as he pulled Ms. Softstone back towards the door.

"Baby come on back in the house."

"Yeah baby, you should listen to your momma."

"Wiz I swear if you don't kill this shit on my step-" Rell said.

"What motherfucker?" Cutty took off around the side of the building as Wiz pulled a long chrome pistol from his waistband. The sun caught the side of the gun and threw light into Rell's eyes.

"Whatcha gon do player? Whatcha gon do?"

"Mom, Mr. Johnny go back inside please," Rell said calmly. "Look Wiz, I don't want none of your shit man. I just want you to take your business off the porch."

"Rock you ain't shit but a car thief and a punk. I should blow your fucking head off, but I won't. On the other hand."

A shot rang out catching Rell in the arm. He fell into the wall and sank to the ground. Ms. Softstone ran outside.

"You lit bastard."

"Ms. Softstone," Johnny called to her so she wouldn't run out into the gunfire. Johnny then ran outside and helped her with Rell. Wiz stood over them with the gun still cocked, smoke drifted from the shiny barrel. Light broke through the trees above his Wiz's head and fell onto Rell. Blood spurt from the hole and ran down to the ground. Another shot rang out from around the building and Wiz dropped his gun. Falling face forward into the dust, he gurgled softly as he inhaled the dirt. Cutty walked up to Wiz and kicked him in the side.

"That shit is for Eddie and Rock you punk, bitch." Cutty turned and ran. Rell awakened as an ambulance and ten police cars pulled into the projects. He looked at Wiz and tried to stand.

"Just be still," Johnny said. Ms. Softstone ran to the ambulance. As the EMT's placed Rell onto the gurney, he could see the cops pushing Cutty's head into a squad car.

Awful To C

Altogether there were thirty layered slices on each of my arms. Each cut open and filled with blackish-gray colored scabs holding each side of my brown skin together as best as they could. In the dips and cracks of the black and gray, dry red peaked out, like standing water after rain. I could feel each cut although I hadn't seen when it happened or saw who did it. But it didn't matter. On the whole it was another week, a Monday and all Mondays were bad for someone. It just so happened that I was chosen for this. Strapped to some cold table, flat and smooth, I could hear every sound but could see only a sliver of light through the heavy wrapping on my head. The wrapping had to be rubber of some kind cause if and when I wiggled my head it pulled at the hairs like rolling a rubber band down an arm.

The table was a type of light metal that didn't clank much when my nails tapped. My fingers seemed the only part, other than my head, that had any degree of movement. But I didn't want to move that much either because the table in spots felt so cold that it was hot when I flinched. I had flinched so much that I'm sure I'd passed out several times. Only to awaken to some odd fluid too warm/thick to be water splashing on my skin. This strap holding me seemed almost cocoon-like and felt to be only on my joints. Any part of me that could bend except my neck and fingers was locked to that cold, cold slab. My chest heaved as I tried to gather all of my strength and move but nothing. Nothing but heat from every part of me as I tried to inch my way from the table. Raw heat, open flame gas heat, quick and sharp making the cold leave for seconds, only seconds.

Those thirty wounds, and I know there were thirty from the time they started until finish, I counted each one. One whistle and sweep and the flesh in the crease between my chest and shoulder spilled warm and thick inside of the shell. A second whistle and sweep, a chunk sound, over the top of my knee came what seemed hours later. Third whistle, sweep and swipe came on the lower, right side of my stomach in the fleshy part above my hip. There seemed to be only seconds separation in the next twenty seven and the heat from the table was nonstop, sizzling my blood as the trickles rolled slowly down each area on my body that was cut. The sides of my neck and what seemed to be any part of skin above a joint that bent. All except my fingers. Which they kept and donated to science. I had donated my body to this and I'm sure no one ever imagined that when you take someone's life and they kill you for it, You are still alive. No heartbeat or brainwaves, no nothing, but you're still there, feeling heat, pokes, tips of blades creating Y cuts in your chest, you can feel it all. You can feel it until you die and wake up over and over.

Short (Untitled)

"And it is this that has made me."

"Ten times ten is simple mathematics, yet those unaccustomed to even the slightest amount of numbers will find this complicated. One times one becomes a problem of infinite measures if the ears, that hear the question, don't understand the words. Quite a mesmerizing statement can be made by considering a life that has been forced into a corner."

"But what about the fact that she was old enough to stop this? Do we assume that her naiveté is a direct result of abuse?"

I sat in my wooden chair and stared at the shine that the floor created from the metal around the long white tubes reflecting fluorescent light onto the polished surface. It could be that she didn't understand. I continued to take notes. Professor Savul strained as he attempted to rewind the tape. Stroking his chin and bending over the black tape player sitting on the top of the metallic gray overhead projector, he pushed play once again.

"And it is this that has made me."

Disgruntled he walked to his podium and looked out over the class. "We are forced often to perceive red as being synonymous with hate, jealousy, anger..."

The light on the floor seemed brighter today, I was positive that someone had buffed the floor. Definitely, a buffed floor. Why was it so important for him to establish that insanity, sometimes, is only a mask for fear? I always assumed that it was a compromise between the mind and life in general.

"No she couldn't have done it."

This *it* was becoming more of mental burden for me because it seemed logical that her story was obviously a creation to deal with her father's death. There wasn't a key term or phrase that hinted that she was insane.

"A clear case of dementia, strain caused by years of-"

The tape player could work if he took the tape out and tightened it. Have you ever had a tape that wouldn't play? Sometimes the tape has too much slack.

"May I try the tape Professor?"

"Go ahead, I would like for you all to listen again. While you do that, ponder this,"

I walked between Sandy, and Paul, stepping over his shoes onto the slick floor and accidentally stepping on her foot. A small scuff appeared on the floor where her foot was.

"A complicated issue of violence produced by a number and a color, red. Nine-fifty every night for fifteen years, without a day missed. She had become conditioned to lay on her back and stare at the clock on her dresser."

A little more and I bet this tape will work. "I'm good at this kind of thing," I thought as I walked back to my seat.

"Listen closely," Professor Savul pressed the pause button and let it go. I felt proud of making the tape rewind. I took notes.

"In this dream I squeezed the trigger. I placed my small fingers around the grip, put my forefinger into the hole and squeezed the half-moon. I could feel the heat from the barrel as it escaped the long, black muzzle."

"Can you hear how her voice inflection denotes her emotional state? Listen."

I really don't appreciate the way I have to learn how a conditioned response exists as long as the stimulus is present. How can this be presented as a learning tool. Pavlov's dog and this? Principles of behavior notes for the last time.

"Silver smoke drifted from the hole as the gun dropped from my hands onto the floor. His eyes opened, bright and wide. He looked down at the blood pumping from the hole in his chest. He placed his stubby hands over the hole and tried to catch the blood, stop the blood."

"Clearly Professor it is not her current tone that possesses the sound of fear. It seems as if she hates."

"Indeed hate is definitely a response that seems to be captured in her inflection, but it is not hate that drove her."

"It was a systematic response to a condition that had pervaded throughout most of her life? An unconditioned response that didn't seem at all irrational in that she had reverted back to a state of protection," I said.

"Maybe, listen."

It would be a lot better in here if they polished the floors more often, I think it helps the ambiance.

"I felt no sense of justice or anger as he fell forward, his hairy stomach hitting the carpet in an awkward manner. His underwear still around his ankles. The twisted smile through a five day old beard, shifted into an oblong O as he gurgled and swallowed blood. I continued to stand and watch him. My skin, covered in goose bumps, felt warm from the blood that sprayed onto me. In the mirror my body seemed to be a distorted picture, a gross image."

"Doctor may I be excused for a moment?"

"Professor Savul please stop the top and rewind it. I thought I heard something odd in her voice."

"Shifted into an oblong O-"

"There, oblong isn't the word of a person suffering from dementia."

I don't know about this, years of school to sit here and analyze a clear case of-

"Please listen. This patient was an extremely intelligent girl."

I took more notes and looked at the scuff marks the guy in the front of the room was leaving with the heel of his boot.

"My pubic hair matted with red, blood, from the razor blade slices he made. Yet I felt no sense of justice. I stood. In this dream I squeezed the trigger and watched him die."

"Do you all believe this was a dream? That was rhetorical, yes it was a dream to her. What you have to do is separate her dream statements and distinguish the reality within her words. Now, the situation had created, yes"

"Could it be that she created a story that justified what had happened to her?"

"Quite possibly. It could be a fabrication, but never assume or you may lose the main idea of what the patient is attempting to tell you."

Damn if the tape is about voice inflection and whether the words that are being mentioned are *not* true, then what is it that we are attempting to decipher?

Professor Savul walked towards the middle of the room, he looked at us and walked to the board. As the blue marker tapped on the board, I stared at the light that also reflected off the white boards surface.

"Life is only a deceitful pretense in which we create stories to justify our lives. Stories which become true if heard enough, stories which become myths if we are afraid of them." He continued to speak as he wrote two words on the board: Listen/ Hear.

"Turn the tape on for me please."

I walked to the tape and pushed play.

"I prayed that he would die as he lay, humping and grunting. His salty sweat dropping into my mouth as he did shaky push ups on top of me. Mom in the next room crying, but not helping, as if tears would stop him. They hadn't stopped him for the last fifteen years. I tried to go to my special place this time but it didn't work. It didn't work, it didn't work, it didn't work. I clinched my eyes as tight as possible, every time I opened them I could see the veins on my eyelids like a bright light. He grunted louder and louder, I could hear my mother shouting, "Get off of her you bastard, get off, get off." I closed my eyes and her voice faded away. I opened them, saw the flash of light and dad lay still on top of me. His breathing a low gurgle. His eyes rolled back into his head. Mother stood at the door, the hallway light shined like a shroud behind her head. With her left hand she covered her mouth. In the dream I squeezed the trigger, saw the light flash, my ears rang as I watched them die."

"What did her voice tell you? Was the patients voice afraid, angry, what? Understand that this is the story of a woman who has been institutionalized for over five years. Can you hear any regret in her voice?"

"Is that the end of the tape?"

"No, what is it?"

"I believe she has created a story of part truth, part fiction. All true and yet not really what happened."

"No ambiguity, please."

I laughed at her statement. She was attempting to be intelligent, but didn't even know what she was saying. I give better answers when I don't pay attention. Excuse me Professor,

"The environment, probably a sterile environment where she has been held and obviously medicated, has created in the patient a sense of control. Which is good because she has at least come to grips with the death of her parents."

"And?"

But now that she has come to this point, it is the job of the staff and her psychiatrist to help her find the truth in her own statements.

"Very good. Understand it is her environment and medication that has elicited this story. Once we realize that our surroundings are the predicators of our actions then we can help the patient. It really wasn't voice inflection I wanted you to hear. It was the analysis of all of the notes on the board, the handouts and this tape."

Venting

"On your left is Hustler's Heaven. The place to find that cloud with the silver lining, you know the cloud of white smoke attached to Junkies Alley over there to your right. You don't know what junkies alley is?

Let's take a tour. One that began on a boat ride, a long middle passage boat ride. Look at the bareback brothers and sisters hiding over there. All huddled together in groves, unable to move for fear that the zoo keeper will come and take away their heaven. Look at em.

Oh, I'm sorry this is the end of this section but look at our new edition. Uncle Tom's car lot, where only the finest automobiles this side of this city can park. Cadi's, Monte Carlos, Regal's the cars of kings. Those are the rulers and maintainers of Hustler's Heaven and Junkie's Alley.

Yeah brother we can get you feelin fine, what you need a five or a dime? For a twenty you can have a piece of Gibraltar my man."

Weed head's find peace in mellow madness and silver haze that daze and create a deceitful atmosphere, and I fear the repercussions as time passes and weed no longer has an effect on them. What next my brother? What next?

Timeless questions of brotherhood are discussed only when the hood is shot to pieces. We don't kill you, we kill we, and it's this ironic place where we dwell when a man is consider a man because of his hair and fashion. A drug dealer and a hypocrite are the same person. I've pulled kids out of gangs and what did your Rev. Jacksonesque, Muslim rhetoric do for you? It got you lauded by your peers in a place that doesn't really count. Welcome to Hustler's Heaven and Junkies Alley, where weed is the word and gettin high means you reached a respectable status within your click. Have you ever lived in any world other than your own? Other than the worlds you've created in your poems. Things are bad here, yet time and words are wasted on Africa, when America is in arms. Fighting is not a last resort it is the only resort. Not a physical fight but a mental fight where the lines are no longer blurred by intraracial racism. Intraracial disrespect.

Perm or fro, waves or dreads don't make you, dashikis or ties don't separate you, for your true identity will always stare you in the face when you awaken in the morning and catch a glimpse of your soul in a mirror. What have you really done for your people today? Did you talk to a child about education, give a brother a hand, did you listen? What have you really done for your people? Or did you write words on a piece of paper and present a theory spoken on a college campus or in a coffeehouse, a theory that is just a theory. Never spoken where they are needed, never spoken to the kids.

In This Patient's Eyes

(Twenty Years)

In the distance Our Father's Hospital towers in Metropolitan City, U.S.A. The movement of the morning pedestrians creates a twisted path of hats and colors down the crowded street. The hospital is an older structure that has been updated to retain it's original form, which was a cathedral. Ruby red, stained glass windows in the hospital reflect the light the sun is casting through the trees from across the street in the park. It is a heavenly vision. The abundance of green and brown vines crawling up the old, white walls of the hospital look as if they were painted onto the surface.

Each of the steps towards the front of the hospital is bordered by a well maintained bed of flowers. The large oak doors of the entrance are open, through them I can see the polished marble columns lining the passageway. The sidewalk in front of the entrance is extremely worn from years of neglect. The hospital continues to look as beautiful as it did when it was a cathedral. As I weave through several stationary people, I notice the large cross that sits at the peak of the building. It makes me feel at ease. I lay myself down. The pain in my chest is unbearable; surely someone will help an old, vagrant woman. Surely, the good Dr. will help. I huddle against the cornerstone of the two foot wall that holds the flower bed in place.

On the bronze placard, in the flowerbed, there is a saying, "Life is sacred. There is love and care for all who seek it." I lie underneath the sign. People walk by staring at the lines and wrinkles in my face that barely hide the look of despair in my blue eyes. My hair blows gently in the morning breeze as small dust tornadoes cover my feet with soot from the passing vehicles. Draped in what was once a beautiful, white choir robe, all that remains of my heavenly garment is stained with urine and dirt. I double over, writhing in pain. I reach out slowly to grab the legs of several nurses who have just arrived for their morning shift; but the nurses continue to walk.

My eyes follow them as they disappear into the entrance. The sound of engines running, horns blowing, people cursing, talking and laughing covers my voice and turns each of my phrases into a slight mumble. I attempt to increase my volume to gain someone's attention. Simultaneously, I reach for each person that walks by, "Please, will you please help."

Several children run by and kick my arm. They laugh as they continue on. As they run out of view, I notice the black, luxury car move into the busy turn lane. The license plates read DRISIN. Looking over the long hood I notice that the driver is a hefty Black man with short, curly hair. His glasses sit low upon his broad nose. After he pushes his glasses back into the correct position, which he has to do continuously, I can see that he is belting out the tune that's playing on his radio. Holding the steering wheel with both hands; his fingers tap to the rhythm. He nods his head as he checks his rear view mirrors and looks ahead to ensure that it's safe to turn. He is my doctor, my savior.

As he parks his car, he reaches over to grab his white coat. He gets out of the car continuing to hum and sing. His large frame moves gracefully between the masses of people towards me, and the front entrance.

I reach out.

The Dr. continues to walk not recognizing that I am in need. His feet dance to the sound of his voice, which is attempting to stay even toned. I snatch his pants leg, he backs away quickly, breathing heavily, looking down at me.

"What the hell are you doing. Move, move ... let me go."

He moves away from me and tries to make his way into the hospital. I realize that the placard has lied. I call out in the strongest voice I can muster, "Dr. please save me. I need you to save me. There is so much that needs to be done. So much work to complete."

"Take your filthy hands off of me. Damn homeless people always asking for shit. Why don't you go clean yourself up or something."

He begins to walk away. I push myself into an upright position to show him the large gaping wound between my breast. Each time I breath, blood flows from the gash. The dusty robe is clinging; connected by dry, brown, blood that is being replaced by a new pool of the fluid. He notices that there are layers to my wound. He kneels down to look closer. I speak to him softly in his ear, "Dr., you owe me. Please help me. I have helped you so many times. You need me... don't let me die."

He stares at me confused. Kneeling down in front of me he speaks with a puzzled look on his face. "What do you mean I owe you?"

I shift my weight slightly, causing the blood to pump out once again onto my clothing.

"Oh Jesus. Just, just hold on mam; lie still."

Startled at the amount of blood, he rocks backwards falling onto his behind. He notices that there are maggots and flies around my wound. Standing and turning away he says, "Mam, I need to get you inside. I'll be right back."

As the Dr. turns towards the stairs he looks back and notices that I am smiling. I feel that he can sense that my smile, bright and warm, is coming from a place that is cold and empty. He stops and kneels down once again and asks, "Why do I owe you? You said I owe you, why? Who, who are you?"

"I am only a concerned friend." I allow my voice to regain strength and authority as I speak to him. "I have watched you grow into a fine young man. I can recall when you were ten years old."

Staring at me intensely, he bites his lip, and switches from one knee to the other. People continue to walk by, bumping him and causing him to lose his balance. He looks deeper and deeper into my eyes.

Through my eyes he can see his mother sitting at a small fold - up dinner table. She has several letters in front of her. She is running her fingers through her hair and mumbling to herself. He can see himself as a young boy running into the room.

I'm sure he remembers the moment, his mother had refused to give him money for candy.

"Remember when your mom had just finished paying the bills? You wanted money to spend on dumb, meaningless, frivolous things... and poor, broke, hands covered with calluses to take care of her only child, mother said that *yaw'll   couldn't afford to spend no money*. You were upset when you ran to your room weren't you?"

He can see himself running down a long hallway that has a wall furnace and three rooms. The last door begins to open slowly. His young eyes become fixed on the door. He looks back towards the kitchen with a look of apprehension in his eyes. With each of his steps he moves slower and turns back towards the door that is opening. The room is his mother's. He can see her purse on her nightstand.

"You just didn't believe her so I helped you find out the truth." He interrupts my story, grabbing me and questioning,

"Old woman what the hell are you saying? If I was in my right mind I would leave you here."

"But you are in your right mind, as you were then. You walked into your mother's room and saw her purse. There were five dollar bills sticking up. You took two. I opened the purse for you. I helped you, I showed you the way and you followed like all good disciples do."

"How, did you know that? Who are you?"

I smile at the terror that shows in his expression. He fixes his eyes upon mine once more and realizes that the whites of my eyes are now bloodshot. I continue to speak to him.

"Not just yet, you will know who I am shortly. We have worked so well together. I must say, you are an excellent pupil. In medical school you found yourself unable to study, I kept sliding that little guys paper, that sat in front of you over on the desk so you could see it."

Visibly shaken, my good Dr. drops to his knees. I can hear the noise in the city pick up, so I wave my hand silencing the crowd. The sun falls down upon the Dr. as he drops his head in a state of utter confusion. He once again looks up into my eyes. When he attempts to make eye contact with me, I cause an eye looking from within my wound, covered by blood to blink.

I exhale loudly to regain his attention. "I had to come to you, I've been hurt. Please help me. I don't mean to torture you with these stories of your past. I just want you to know that I have helped you and I honestly believe that it is your duty to help me. If it weren't for me, the alcohol you drink to erase the memory of the patient you allowed to die, would be useless." I stare at him compassionately and stroke the hair on his head, "Don't cry my child."

He lifts his head and wipes his tears away, the traffic freezes, and the city becomes motionless, time has stopped for this moment. The only movement is myself and the Dr. He looks at me and questions, "Why should I help you if you allowed me to do all of those things? You should suffer and die. You deserve to die!"

I look at him; my eyes are once again white and full of despair. I lie down, my voice becomes weak again. He moves closer, unwillingly, to hear my revelation.

"I have existed forever, but for me to continue, every twenty years I have to reveal myself. I have to be saved by human souls who know who I am. Without me there wouldn't be a need for hospitals. No need for technology. Individuality would be unnecessary. All people would be equal. Where would the jobs be?" I pause allowing this to sink in. I understand that the idea of Satan needing to be saved is hard to accept, I have always had to convince people.

"Existence would be meaningless without death, greed, envy, and beauty. Would you want to live in a world that had no purpose except to breed and live?"

He staggers away from me. I allow the stillness swirling around him to stop as I breathe my last few breaths. I extend my hand to him once again. I can sense the horror and helplessness overcoming him as I ask him for the last time,

"Will you help me? Do you think you should make the decision as to how the rest of the world should live?" I ask angrily. "Look at them, they're happy and content. Your selfishness would take that away. Save my life and the world will continue as it is. You will be successful beyond your dreams. Will you help me?"

The Dr. finally stands to reach for my hand. When he touches me, several young men ram him. He looks to see if I am still lying in front of him. There isn't any reason for me to stay, he has done his part. I move swiftly down the street as he looks for me in every direction. Through the crowd, I allow him to glimpse me standing on the corner.

As expected, he runs towards me shouting. I complete his torture by stepping off the curb into the onslaught of traffic. As I remove myself from the body of the vagrant, a car slams into the woman. Her lifeless body flips over the hood and through the windshield. People gather around the car. The doctor runs to the woman and attempts to help, but it's too late. The crowd of people begin to shout, "He was chasing her. He made her do it, he made her do it."

The good doctor shakes his head realizing what he has done, "I didn't do it. I was trying to help her."

The crowd continues to yell. I smile as the Dr. drops to his knees, and looks up at the sky with his arms outstretched, shouting "Why."

I answer, so only he can hear, "Another twenty years my son, another twenty years."

Poetry

Section 1: Invisible

Writing Black:

Rhythms found in repetition

and the musical placement of sounds

of words that lay together

like sheet music spooned into

black folders, filled like rivers

after rain.

Not vague.

Blacks have a more defined goal:

To relate experiences common to

the insular ghetto.

Situations in which the Negro

lives and like an animal

grows an affinity towards.

Cops, beat downs, sit-ins,

uproars, metaphysical, voodoo,

anger, Africa...

Ghetto born, ghetto death.

Is this how you write Black?

Burkle Estate

I remember things:
Where the field sat in front of the gym
and seemed to grow green for miles,
the path behind our homes
that ran between trees
and was so worn it looked like
a path for cars,
and Grant Elementary,
the school I attended as a child.

All of those things have changed.
Bricks sit and tall weeds grow;
dying placeholders for memories.

I remember things:
Now I see this place differently.
The neighborhood I created
and its true history.

Childhood made 200 yards of street seem like miles.
We rarely ventured beyond our self-imposed
parental boundaries.
When we did, we did so for the adventure,

never noticing signs or certain homes.

I am 31 now. I drive my wife
and 1 year old son through Memphis
to show them where I was raised.
I drive all over, through the boundaries.

I see raised placards
that in my childhood
I never noticed.

I was never told, when I went to Grant ,
that less than a block away from 5th street,
slaves slept under this house where men sought work.
The Underground Railroad ran through my backyard.

Fireplugs on Summer Days

1

Cracked sidewalks cascaded like branches
of rivers into chipped spaces of jagged rock.
Hot pavement left pebble prints in the
soles of bare feet. Black, brown, cream, all
shades of children switched feet, danced
a heat inspired hopscotch, upon
blacktop painted with patched potholes.
Seldom used swim trunks stuck to
sweaty legs, legs too short to walk
to public parks, legs long enough
to pace Fifth Street. I waited to cool
down from water from fireplug spouts.
I never noticed the looks on faces back then.

2

The fireplugs sit dry on North Fifth today.
Weeds grow through the cracks in the pavement now.
No children's jubilant jump rope routines,
No 1,2,3, red light or street football,
No bikes riding too fast down project hills.
Red boards block windows on closed tenements.
Rust colored bricks hide the names from childhood.
Names like Tone, Smoke and Stack, still living there.

North Fifth what happened? Did cold winter nights,
Hot summer days, twist and chip your painted skin
from homes, and the people, I saw today?
The faces watching from those porches
don't sing childhood songs... unknowingly carefree.
They look abandoned, sitting with forties and cards.
Or was it that way when I was a child?

Section 2: Street

After Reading a Bronzeville Poem

I first saw the picture of Emmitt Till when I was about ten years old. I think it was in a Jet or some other Magazine. I knew what it was. I knew why it was there. I even understood why he was murdered. I found anger then. I was a ten year old boy in Memphis. I was being bussed to an all White school in a North Memphis suburb and I thought White people smelled funny. I never liked the bus ride. I found anger but never questioned any White folks at the school about the picture. I played games and learned. I looked at the picture and couldn't imagine looking like that. I got older. My grandmother died that year. My mother returned. We moved. I didn't get bussed again. I wish I could remember how that picture made me feel then. Now I have manufactured a disgust and hatred for the men who killed him. But what's sad is that I write of James Byrd and Amadou Diallo now. Not much has changed.

Projects

Proposed policies place protective prevents, Posing perplexing problems pushing people past permanent placards positioned plentifully

Throughout terrible tenements tainting the thoughts that touch those true to themselves.

How harsh history holds, hampers, hinders, honest hearts helps humans

Understand?

Brooks on Wright

Bigger and the boys,

afraid of taking white, sit and sip

on cheap spirits,

smoke old squares

from others ashtrays,

whistle with feet against the wall.

Live past the summer and await the fall.

A Response to a Letter

If you give your Black back,

you would have to give up sucking your fronts after eating pork ribs

and drinking a forty on a hot ass Sunday in the backyard

of baby brothers house on the corner of MLK and

Jackson Street, while listening to the Isley brothers, and the OJays talk

about "Money" in the projects while your lit sister got her hair

straightened with royal crown grease in the kitchen

where your lazy ass uncle fell asleep after eating his ribs

and sneaking a drink out of the purple crown royal bag

you kept your marbles in.

Hey how come the Black Back didn't say anything about not giving my fatback,

pig feet and chittlins back?

Must have been a Muslim that wrote it

Hell I ain't givin back my corn bread either,

and what about ketchup sandwiches or molasses sandwiches

and Blaxploitation movies, I'll be damned if someone takes

my copy of Goldie or Superfly.

Awww, I forgot If I had to give Shaft back

I would have to shut my mouth forever, can you dig it?

The Street

Passing by several people on the street, I overheard

the words villain, robber, crook and thief.

In disbelief, I paused and stood motionless.

The dust on the sidewalk

kicked up into the air as the wind

from automobiles grabbed each particle

and flung them at the face of the thief, robber, villain.

I was willing to forget the words to avoid the confrontation,

but my frustration overwhelmed me with feelings of hatred.

In a moments notice my mind's eye struck out

and consumed each of them with hell's fire and damnation.

The feelings that burned within me

created visions of middle passage deaths,

lynching in southern states, controlled fates

and slave trade debates;

which all seemed to relate

to the moment I thought about lashing out.

Instead, I stood, they noticed,

I stood, they noticed, I stood

and

they

noticed.

Their laughter and smiles, were replaced by fear and apprehension,

there was dissension in their ranks.

The taller woman turned and walked away,

the smaller man turned and said good day.

The heavy woman clutched her purse without delay;

and I stood.

My Brooks Brothers suit and Kenneth Cole shoes deceived me.

Because according to those people, I was still a color.

My Rolex watch began tick, instead of sweep.

I felt defeat and in a subtle manner

I dropped my head.

A second passed and at last they were on their way.

The dust settled as I stood and wondered why.

With eye's like daggers, I continued down the street,

I continued .....down .....the street.

I want to right a happy poem

Have you ever noticed that there aren't many happy poems?

Most poetry speaks of heartache and failed tasks,

some speak of travel and the days that have passed.

But the point of poetry seems to be expressing misfortune and failed romance.

You see, the ability to create always seems to take a back seat

until we find hardship, or do things that are to remain discrete.

So why is it so hard to write a happy poem?

It's easy to write songs that speak of love,

and claim the gifts from heaven above;

but it's rare to talk of friends and honesty

or what it feels like to be debt free.

Now that would be a happy poem.

To help a child learn to do math,

to help a person down the right path,

to read a book in a hospital ward,

not to condemn preferences and blame it on the Lord.

That would be a happy poem.

I want to right this happy poem,

but to write a poem that's happy means that it has to come from that type of moment.

What starts as a happy line becomes trapped in wrong words and bitter memories.

I want to right a happy poem, but I can't because I feel that I'm wrong.

To write a happy poem one must be content and sure that the moment is right.

I want to write a happy poem, but until I feel all right, I'll continue to write what's left.

The Poet

I no longer fit the role of poet.

No longer.

No clothes too baggy or ratty

tattered and torn

to show that my words are born

of some man's oppression.

I no longer look the part of a poet.

No African garb or braids, plaits

no locks in my hair,

no Afro with a pick jabbed deep into

the coarseness

so many folks describe as chains.

I no longer sound that part of a poet.

No draaaaawn ouuutttt dictations and

lingering highs at the end of sentence

fragments.

I no longer sound like a poet.

No deep resonating well-practiced style

that identifies me with

a longing to be from Harlem, Brooklyn

or some other city under

solstice influenced rhythms.

I no longer hear the words of poetry.

Those words that sound good together

placed in some funky use of

alliteration that rolls off the tongue

making the crowd go ooh....ahhh.

I no longer hear the words of poetry.

Those words of poems that make you say

Amen or snap fingers in a circle with a twist.

Those words full of venom from mouths who haven't

even started to live, only

oppressed by parents and close friends.

I no longer play the part of poet.

Like God

I am.

7 and 21

7

A lucky number signifying

the rattle and roll of white dice falling onto

concrete streets from ashy Black hands.

21

representing flat, shiny aces and kings

in the hands of fiends

looking to hit blackjack.

7

to me means death and birth

for what it's worth

7 August 1971 his baby brother died

living his life for revolution.

21 signifying loss and reincarnation.

21 August 1971

there was Blood in his eye

as our Soledad Brother

shackled and chained

behind rusty, half painted

steel bars was shot down like

an animal in a concrete wilderness.

21 August, gaurds feigned

that he attempted to escape.

Can you blame him?

Could you live knowing each day
is your last?
A dead man can only write of what he is,
the irony is he had no reason to escape.
21 August 1971
George Jackson died at the hands
of a system that said he was a
coon, a monkey,
but can a monkey read theories of Mao
and Marx?
17 October 1971
I arrived. My mother told me
that every time someone dies
someone is born.
Maybe I'm meant to carry on
for George. I start by saying
I am not a nigger, brother,
don't ever call me that.

In A Matter of Minutes

41 rounds fired from sixteen-shot clips.
When you were trained wasn't one shot enough?

Posing as purveyors of good,
assuming that the media hype of
not guilty can cure your conscience.

New York, New York, Big City
of lost dreams,
and language barriers
that cause death.

Whizzing screams of rapid fire
Shattered glass, riddled bricks,
the ground became painted with bloodstains.

And clutching a wallet, Amadou died.

Whistling screams of rapid fire
Shattered glass, bullets riddled the bricks
and fell, onto bloodstained concrete.

Words are not enough to conquer
a task force on a mission.

Yet, I sit wishing
an execution squad
would do the same shit to you.

Whizzing screams of rapid fire,
Shattered glass,
riddled bricks dropped
into bloody puddles on the ground.
Clutching a wallet, Amadou died,
And yet, you were justified?

Wallets and Other Mistakes

His voice soundin' like dance calls,
"Step on out. Get out, an' get on down."
Down and dirty, low enough to see ants
in sidewalk cracks.
City streets covered in his footprints,
Fat knuckles drag concrete,
His badge glistens.
He's Grendel with a shield.
Face wrinkled, eyebrows arched,
thick moustache framin angry words,
florshiems kickin guts, askin' questions later.
You dig?

"I ain't feelin this here beat."
So he tappin new sounds with his nightstick,
head and ribs replace poundin of drums.
Fillin the chamber with clickety clack,
he be takin aim at anyone of color.
Lackin reason,
layin down the law, he
afraid of Timberlands and baggy jeans,
khakis and Chuck Taylor's,
that own nothin.
Unafraid of suits and white collars

costin the nation millions.
Crack pushin... smokin... equals two years,
Ounce of coke: a fine and drug rehab for a month
at your facility of choice.
Neither's right, but rights are read
differently.

Motherfucker got this feelin and figured
I'm too po to have a nice ride.
Pulled me over cause the light was yellow,
asked to search my car.

I got this feelin I'm goin down
for not starin right.
I say a prayer,
as my briefcase sparkles chrome-like
from sunlight
and clickety clack fills the chamber.

Harvesting In Jasper

My fear, finds its ground, on dark Texas streets
where air constricts from ropes stretched tight like
stems.
Lady Day sang of Strange Fruit years ago,
Yet, I revisit the scene still today.

> *Pastoral scene of the gallant south,*
> *The bulging eyes and the twisted mouth,*
> *Scent of magnolias, sweet and fresh,*
> *Then the sudden smell of burning flesh.*

Far removed from the cloak of giant trees,
the harvest takes place on dark, and dusty roads.
A man struggles to keep pace with a truck.
He fails and skips on jagged stones that scrape
his Black skin from his bones. Blood trails behind
the White truck that speeds for almost two miles.
A man harvested in Jasper today
slowly dies like strange fruit hung from limbs.

In Winds Of Rebellion

We dun work these fields from sun up to sun down
In dis place de Lawd dun made
Tired of workin dis land from sun up to sun down
in dis here place de Lawd dun made

Black bodies hold the bushels in bruised hands,
Man, woman, child, wet with heat from humid air.
Cracks from massa's whip, are too much to withstand,
Defiant, and frustrated, he whispered *'enough'*.

No Mo Auction Block For Me

Wind whistles as the air splits from leather,
for one last time, as disobedience
becomes angry mutiny with cries and hollers.
Like dark streaks, Blacks scatter, hide, scream, fight.

He reaches for splintered wood which still burns
along with shucked husks being used as kindle.
He holds the fire to the stalks, and packed bushels.
The fields are set aflame by his strong Black hands.

Can you smell the smoke drifting overhead?
The fields now charred, red in bloody colors,
Heavy gray smoke floats through the autumn sky,
Ash from burnt stalks settles onto shoulders.

In fields, sweat covers yellow stalks of corn.
Blood coats trees on old tobacco roads.
Rows of cotton echo Negro spirituals
of sun blackened backs carrying heavy loads.

Can you smell the smoke drifting overhead,
Snatching the air from my soul as I breathe?
Rolling flames singeing green grass, burning homes,
Each spark following the first fires lead.

In fields, we stood and watched the smoke drift off,
we stood and stayed there until the last flame
consumed chains holding us from true freedom.
Do you see the smoke setting free our names?

We dun work these fields from sun up to sun down
In dis place de Lawd dun made
Tired of workin dis land from sun up to sun down
in dis here place de Lawd dun made

Section 3: Headlines as Art

The Death of Chivalry

I looked for symbols and metaphors

to describe what you've done.

I sought a comparative situation,

but became typical in my thoughts,

"If a Black man had done this to someone..."

But that's not the issue, cause

tragedy is what it is and the color makes all stop.

Maybe your conviction for burglary,

petty theft,

DWI,

maybe seeing Black families

decimated by 3 strike laws

gives me the right to say,

"If a Black man..."

But this was someone's son

who was murdered, taken by

a Jack Daniel, Seagram, commercial driven liquor

binged right cross

and this ain't about Black,

it ain't about a White man getting 3 years

for involuntary manslaughter,

it ain't about your cicada shelled apology

to David Govito's mother,
it's not about you J.Brick.

It is about a man who wondered
if he would die for a cause.
David I don't know you, your family,
but I will remember.

Firing Squad

The video game has a reset button.
Schoolwork can be retested.
The government can reconsider laws
but life...
One a White supremacist, one a rapist
both murderers. There are 2 of you dying.
To write of one doesn't diminish
the acts of the other.
Though the bloodshed and number murdered is greater.
I write you first Troy Michael Kell.
You who pride your White skin,
White ways,
plunged a homemade knife through brown skin
over and over and over until you
watched every second in the minute plus seven,

you chose death.

You, Robert Arguelles, who raped 4,
tore your mother's insides out:
2 dead little girls, a woman
and one other girl who you stabbed
40 times.
How did you find so many places to dig your
knife into?
Was your stabbing a blind random thing,
or the same place each cut?

Troy and Robert your faces sit on
flimsy, off white paper, non-blinking,
cold stares in shades of black, gray, white.
Headlines stating that you will die
by firing squad.
The law still on the books in Utah.
5 men will shoot, 1 with a blank,
from 30 feet away.
They will live with your death.
You'll be gone and in death
add
5
new

bodies

to your lists.

Headlines as Muse

In San Jose

A one year old

drowns in a pail

his mother filled.

Water for them,

him, his sister,

to play games in.

She only left

for a moment.

In syllabics

I write (wonder)

if art should be

drawn from headlines.

Section 4: Native

Birdsong

1

Blow your sax Charlie.
Push the pads so lids
can open and close
letting air twist through
the brass and escape
each hole in the form
of a note that you
find just as pleasing
as a painting of
you and Dizzy G.
in a Verve session.
When your lips kissed the
reed they found the same
high you sought in dark
rooms away from the
spotlight that calmed your
anxiety of
performing in front
of demanding crowds
expecting you to
be flawless, perfect,

like studio takes
placed on forty-fives.
Why was L.A. your
downfall? You weren't the
same when you returned
to New York to play
with Dizzy at the
famed Savoy Ballroom.
Go ahead and blow
Yardbird and find peace.

2

Quiet ax. Kerouac's muse,
still high, dead, and shit...
I don't know you Charlie.
Found you while,
listening to NPR
one hot afternoon.

They said you was great,
I'd never heard of you.
My momma didn't play jazz,
she lived jazz, bad and good
and struggle ain't half
the word for what she did.

Who cares though?
I discovered you while
sitting, stuck in a funk,
2000 miles from home
wondering why my momma
didn't play jazz.

Knowing why she played
gospel, I now play you
for the same reason.

I ain't as high as you was
and I never will be.
I write about you cause
mom and I both hated
the same man, who,
like you, drugged
himself out of this life.

1

Coltrane's Eyes,

Seek sounds within structured scales.
He sought notes born on undiscovered planes.
His mind strained to make music charts
of past compositions merge into a frame
containing old riffs and newfound chords.
His brow, furrowed above a piercing glance
epitomized an era: artists who strived
to give jazz a texture that would advance
the artform and make improv accepted.
Trane's eyes inspire, making you believe in
the God he sought to reach with his tenor.

Can you compare the soul of jazz music?
The earnest moves of fingers closing valves,
tapping symbols softly to create highs,
black and white keys vibrating strings produce
sounds, melodic waterdrops on windows.
Can you compare the sound of soul music,
forgotten music from tarnished brass?
An undiscovered note comes from within.
Heavy baritones hypnotize with chants,
"*A Love Supreme, A Love Supreme*," a love.

2

And now I stare into my eyes in the morning.
Dark brown eyes, squinting, straining
to see in my face a look that made you run away.

I hold my son, his eyes smile and I think,
'If I could've looked like him
there was no way you would've left.'

But my eyes, face, both darker, was that it?
My lips bigger, hair nappier, was that it?
Did my eyes, like my son's stare too much
and question the beard, moustache, the lines
at the corners of your eyes?
No... My son doesn't know anything.
I don't remember anything from that time,
I can't possibly. I was a child with eye's
that couldn't hypnotize you.

Facade of a Songbird

1

A profile of elegance and beauty,
a facade captures your better side.
Gone too soon, a voice that complimented
pianos and horns in be bop nightclubs.
This Lady sang the Blues passionately,
eyes closed vocal chords tense bellowing jazz.
The sound of a God given instrument,
The power of pictures belying truth.
The truth: a once beautiful voice,
that sang of strange fruit and shattered hearts,
cracked like broken mirrors in back alleys.
Reduced to midnight sets for change,
in exchange, for no longer hidden habits.
Gone too soon, a songbird taking flight on
iron lines. Needles filled with pasty brown,
melted over flames slowly, shaking, until the
fluid becomes hidden in veins no longer found
without tying rubber around your limbs.
Gone too soon, the songbird of Harlem.

2

You must've looked like a peacock
to mom. You know what I'm sayin:
that strut...head high, breast out,
brass gold, blood red, sky white and blue,
shit all kinds of hues on wings
opened, ain't that how peacocks
get theirs?
Your arms spread, eyes to the sky,
smooth as hell.
Yeah, you had to look like a peacock.
And I figure mom couldn't see you
for all them colors.
Hell, even I stare at the peacocks
at the zoo, that shit is beautiful.
But mom couldn't see past that.
She stared a little bit too long.
Your Chicago, big city style,
all peacock and not a fucking thing else.

A Snapshot of Miles

1

The drums seem tall towering over the crowd.
Muted shades of black and gray, with flashes
of white light shroud cymbals on narrow stands.
This snapshot of Miles, I imagine captures the passion,
the soul, the sound of *Moon Dreams*, *Kind of Blue*.
Sounds produced by moistened lips pressed against
a gleaming trumpet clutched by long black
fingers releasing valves, moving air through the brass.
Recognition's caught in the eyes of grainy figures,
an audience held captive by high pitched
bleats that pierce the air. In a spirit filled club
in L.A., cameras flash, lights make silhouettes
behind Miles as a halo finds a home on the crown
of a jazz saint inventing the sound of cool.

2

I have only one picture of you. And damn...
you look elegant, honest, and all that other shit
you claim to be. Then again, I have several
pictures of you, but they all make your ass
seem like a Motown song. You know,
"Whenever you call me, I'll be there. I'll be around."
I mean, those pictures... you was decked out!
Clean, in three piece suits, Stacy's, hat tilted
over one eye, Bible in hand.
The flash of the camera catching just a glimpse
of your style. The camera didn't do you justice.
Even in color the real you didn't come through.
I have a few pictures of you.
I got them from you.. when I was nineteen.
I acted like everything was cool.
But father, we got miles between us.

A Jig With Monk

1

Black and whites rise and fall
with the stress of fingers pushing.
Mallets press strings, tightly woven hairs,
stretched inside the belly of a Baby Grand.
In 52nd Street nightclubs he played
polyrhythmic notes
created by African percussions.
His hands drifted above the keys
searching for the last line of music
to bring everyone to their climax.
Sounds overlapping,
Silhouettes shrouded in smoke,
clap to complicated layers of *Cris Cros*sing
between routines, and inspiration.
The master and his slaves, hypnotized,
united, in once segregated halls,
by the combination of black and whites,
like fingers interlaced, keys drop hammers
on taut strings in the belly of a Baby Grand.

2

Thelonius refused to play before he died.
His hands still able to press and create
patterns of plinking, plunking, disjointed sounds
found their seventh day and rested.

You, not like Thelonius, never played for me.
Never, not on Monday, Thursday, or Saturday
did you take your mind and hands and create
life within a breath created by your lust.

I listen to Thelonius for inspiration when I write.
I listen to you and like a gutted piano your
songs sound hollow, devoid of hammers
striking the right chords, just an empty shell.

Thleonius refused to play before he left,
deservedly so. He left us with so much.
You refused to play before I could speak one
word. Thelonius inspires me more than you.

Dizzy

1

The flashing streaks
from comet tails,
diving dolphins
swimming beside
Navy vessels,
The sound from your
trumpet those notes
of be bop jazz and
gunfire at the
end of games won,
are much too brief.

A picture shows
your forefinger
pressing your lips,
your jaws expanding
look like balloons
above your chin.
Memorable,
Legendary
that sound and style
of yours is, still.

2

My son bounces on his knees,
holds on to the edge of anything
dipping and rising
like weight lifters finishing squats,
and this is happiness.
He bounces at the end of the bed
holding the rail,
He pulls pieces of Shakespeare
from the bookshelf and eats them,
and this is happiness.
Chubby cheeks prepped
for future jazz bleats on trumpet,
now full of ga ga, da da, na na,
ma ma,
full of wet kisses.

Crawling throughout the house,
I chase behind to make sure he's
safe.
Listening to Dizzy,
while watching him,
is
happiness.

Son To Father

Today I found myself thinking of you.
Why this occurred I honestly don't know.
It happened around 4 p.m. walking through
red lights, and across streets where traffic flowed.
Cars at a standstill, sun refracting off windows,
and a small breeze, somehow brought other thoughts
to my mind although there were things I ought
to have been focused on, like talking with my boy.

Why was it so damned easy for you to walk off?
Did my birth scare you, bring the end of youth?
I walk with my son down streets and I pause
his small hands in mine, his expression aloof
he doesn't see what I see, doesn't know loss.
Today, I found myself with thoughts of you.

Son to Father 2

Sitting alone under this
lantern, loose cannon holding
still. Street lights blinking.
A loose cannon under lanterns
of dark stairwells, around crack sells,
Memphis was hell, so I left behind a loose cannon
who died under a street light,
alone, alone. Under the shine of blue and red,
Twisting dance lights, moving atop black and white
holding me captive, a loose cannon detained.
Eyes burn behind thoughts.
Distant screams from within, captured.

I hate how you and your generation
shitted on our mothers and fucked
all of us up so bad that we won't
marry or be responsible.

At this point,

I'm beginning to open.

I can't bring certain questions

into my mouth. I'll write them.

You are growing old:

Gray hair, thick stomach, hands without elastic,

wise words.

I'm teaching myself to hear you, see you.

I don't know how you run:

Short strides, long strides, on your toes,

or did you use the whole foot to push you forward?

I can imagine you walking.

I can see you walking, your shoulders square,

neck leaning like your head hurt,

a slight twitch and sweep of the heels

on grass, concrete.

I know what you look like from a distance.

Your walking eyes though,

I don't know them.

At this point I'm beginning to open.

I expect your calls every Sunday.

I get the phone and attempt to call you,

but I still think this is your job.

I have no 3 year old to 18 year old memories of you.

When you call to speak, like we haven't been apart,

my wife touches my shoulder and sits my son on my lap.

He knows me, calms me. He can make me smile.

I know death is near you.

The telephone is your lap.

I'm hearing you.

I'm 3 years old.

Section 5: Connections

The Last Thirty-Five

The idea was to walk in rhythm, for a purpose,

following Dr. King to the promised land,

A slow stride to freedom.

The idea was to march to the chords

of music ringing out in dispute of wrongs that had occurred,

A slow march to freedom, A slow march to freedom.

What happened to our walks, what happened to our marches?

What happened to us?

Lack of trust?

Content with the times, we allowed ourselves to settle.

The idea was to march and walk our way to equality;

but what happened along the way?

65 killed the Hajj, but pacified us with the Civil Rights Act.

68 murdered Rex, so they confused us with the text that continued the war.

They drafted us to prevent the movement and it worked.

Rainbows pushed and Panthers attempted to rally,

but the numbers were tallied and we found that nothing had changed,

So we became frustrated and settled.

We settled for the Rev. On the Balcony, who survived, to guide us.

The idea was to walk in rhythm, the idea was to march to the chords...

Lack of focus,

Lack of desire?

We began to tire, the projects didn't seem so bad;

at least we could ride the bus.

Lack of trust?

Lack of trust. We yelled Geronimo and they placed him behind bars, decapitated the Panther, and covered it with the

price of gas. We sat on our ass.

They rewarded us, so we didn't fuss, we could go to their colleges.

We let go of the struggle because it wasn't hip to be Black.

Being Brothers and Sisters didn't suit us, so we called each other niggas, and Blaxploitation made that cool.

The idea was to find our freedom, the idea was to give us hope.

The reality was they gave us dope.

I believe I can fly.

Fly away, float away, we accepted that.

In fact, we turned our backs on Blacks and opened our arms to crack.

We inhaled and exhaled, the doors opened;

we had more jobs and the Reverend On the Balcony ran for office.

We forgot to address crack, and the lack of the Black family structure.

The idea was to find our dreams and so it seemed

that we had. Out of the projects a few of us moved,

Well we moving on up,

Up to what? Babies Daddies?

I know the Lord

and the Lord knows you, so what else is new?

When we became content, the government spent their time behind closed doors.

They devised and they schemed and came up with a theme

that would separate you and yours.

Destroy the Black man, better yet let him destroy himself.

Give him a taste of White, give him a taste of wealth.

Other Blacks will get jealous over there in the projects and this will perpetuate, Blacks will waste their time on, ain't no good men and other foolish debates.

They got rid of the Klan and brought in gangs, brothers in blue and red.

Claimed eracism, lied about sexism, switched to Semitism and blamed it on Muslims "rage."

But it wasn't rage, simply put it was wage, the minimum which we received.

The idea was to walk in rhythm, the idea was to march to the chords, We shall overcome,

we shall ...

No longer a need for that song, no need for a struggle;

Shush up. We where we want to be, don't cause no trouble.

Black boy murdered in the projects, Black man murdered in Jasper, and Black leaders are just like Casper.

Shush up. Don't cause no trouble, we where we wanna be.

I said don't cause no trouble boy, we where we wanna be.

Sheets of Sound

Despite the incessant boom of ten inch woofers
that drive the music of my era,
I continue to stride into this place where Bird
makes my soul come alive.
Smoke, drifts, and lingers, creating music
on sheets of thin air.
Filters connected to ashtrays also dangle
from quiet lips. Finger snaps propel the moment
as instruments carry the mood to this place,
in this building, in this room, to my booth.
I admire the combination of lyrics and stacked notes.
The sounds of be bop's hi de ho's,
tie into the brassy vocals of Hip Hop,
creating connections when the bass drops.
Chords commence over timeless patterns,
rising melodies, which pace saxophone solos,
that float so low, the sound becomes a Hummm,
before the voice drops in.
The pitch varies in sync with mechanical percussions,
and fuse; Coltrane and Guru, Branford and Buckshot,
two American flavors, the only original flavors,
both labors of love.
There is love for this sound, as I get down

to midnight sessions at the Five Spot;

mixed with vocals labeled, Hot, Phat and Fly.

Some flew on the wings of vices,

which gave license to others to manipulate,

and debate the faults of the righteous.

But I still continue to dig the rhythm of those familiar whispers.

The rhythm, rhyme and repetition, resounds

radically, and rolls around on the wings

of spirits of the past, and the present.

I listen to the horns finding the notes,

that link spirits with the physical.

Pursed, their lips push air through valves that open;

and close in response to fingers that fire

shots of controlled harmony.

I find pleasure in repeating this process of making

the connection.

Hip Hop in My Thirties

In nineteen eighty three after watching
Beat Street, I purchased the soundtrack and got
my first fold out poster 'Guide to Breakin'
I stood in my room practicing the *wave*.
Moving my bed away from the wall I
tried to perform the backspin exactly
the way the creased fold out poster described.
Crazy Legs, step one: the backspin-leg back,
in that awkward stretch that doesn't really
stretch anything but hurts your knee and back.
I'd rewind the song Planet Rock at least
Twenty times. Every now and then I still
Lay on the floor, leg back, when no one's watching
And try to spin, if only for a minute.

Section 6: Hearth

Missing Memphis

Warmth pulls beads of sweat from pores.
Long fields of grass covered in dipping
dragonflies. At dusk, yellow lights
from flying beetles move through
towers of trees. Street football paused
by yells of, "Car Time".

Summer whispers in my ear of fall.
Changing, leaves, brown, rust orange...
Seasons passing, and my mother's voice.

Like Mom's Soul Food

Soon it will be done, these troubles of the world.
As soft sounds of gospel spiritually uplift,
Mom's voice repeats the phrase between the riffs.
Mahalia reaches for notes to praise the Lord.

Move on up a little higher.
I rise and smile, hearing these sounds I know.
My senses peak. Smells of dinner and echoes
of bowls, pots, stirring, causes me to shift.

Morning air filled with the scent of pepper.
Salt and ground spices filtered through the heat
of an oven baking golden corn bread
and seasoned chicken that's spicy, yet sweet.

Smoked neckbones boil in onions, with bay leaves.
After three hours meat falls from the bone,
tender enough to add in long, collard greens.
Mom adds butter to yams in casserole dishes.

Tempted to sneak in and take a piece of
corn bread, I sense my mom standing behind.
My hand, stinging, moves quickly away from
the bread and completes my childhood routine.

God Shall Wipe Away All Tears.
Things haven't changed, through years I've grown.
Childhood reflections don't wane as you age,
this day reads like a familiar poem.

Amazing Grace, how sweet the sound.
Going home is like turning to the page
of a book that you cherish and hold fast.
This is how I feel when Mahalia is played,
and songs nourish like Mom's soul food.

Section 6: 29 April 03

Dialysis Clinic

I'm writing you.
Don't know if there's a man
where you headed.
Where you're going,
but I don't see a man now
young or old.

You sit looking through 2 layers
of metal and glass doors,
red buttons inside of plates painted
with handicap symbols wait to be pushed
so doors can open and someone,
anyone, whoever, can come
to take you somewhere.

Black hat, black shirt, black skin,
gray hair, black
history in your face.
You are our Black
mother left sitting in the dialysis clinic.

Your head rests on your arms,
wheelchair pushed against the white wall,
bright, polished floors
shadowed by the wheels and your weight
flexes the soft seat toward the floor.

I'm waiting on my mother.
I'm here for her,
thinking of you,
wondering if you know
I'm writing you.
sneaking glances
hoping you don't notice.

The Treatment

A professor once said

that the word love should never be used in a poem.

I love my mother.

In her there are steel flowers bright, polished,

attached with sinews and cartilage.

Flowers held by cold solder joints.

But they've been that way for years, decades.

Finally, they seem ready to crack,

drop to the floor and break like

glass.

I look in your eyes,

we both smile and shake our heads.

"Who would've thought?"

"They should've left it alone."

You always told me

sickle cell should've taken you

years ago.

I didn't see it then.

With the hum and whir

of pumps pushing red through

plastic tubes,

I can't see the shape of your blood cells,

but I see you.

I don't think you need this clinic.

You sit in the chair and smile,

we nod our heads.

Readjustment

Frustration builds
in this aqua turqioise room.
The sliver of a bed
a cheap teevee,
your sterile sheets pulled to your chin.
You drift off.

Patience is not your stronger virtue
and waiting for 3, 4, 7
hours to be cut in the stomach
is worse than the cutting.

But you seem more at ease than usual.
This is why I stayed instead of leaving.
How does my presence help?
Who cares as long as it does.
I know I've been away for years, but I want
to show you that I'm strong;
that you've done a good job.
I think this gives you strength.

Wind Colored Prayers

We will leave soon,

son, grandson, daughter in law

and you will stand in the driveway

waving, telling us to be careful, mouthing

I love you.

I'll hold in tears.

My wife will rub the hair on my arm.

I'll see the glisten in your eye,

a drop of dew on a rose.

You'll be clutching your robe closed with one hand.

We will both thank God,

and send wind colored prayers:

Yours for a safe trip.

Mine for enough years

that you see great grandchildren.

Distance

The brown kitten sits in the tree.
Clots stick to her matted fur.
Claws clutch seams in branches
grayish, black bark like ridges.
She mews into a southern wind
that tosses yellow veined leaves
to the ground far below.
I stand, not straining to see,
But distant enough that I can't reach.
I have a ladder not long enough,
I have words that only ricochet
Through the breeze.
Here I stand twenty feet
From a bleeding kitten,
What can I do to help you
When I am so far away.

You would've loved Ray.

"I'ma make it do what it do."

You would've loved this movie.

Every moment of watching the film

I thought about how much you enjoyed simplicity

You liked your heating pad in the bed,

You liked your tea in the morning

It used to be coffee until you started getting sick.

You liked to watch the Golden Girls

And you liked watching the old black and white movies.

Yeah, I'm quite certain you would've loved watching Ray.

I cried several times thinking about that as

I watched.

Section 7: Langston

Ain't no Aunt Sue's no more.

When fall comes down settlin on trees and leaves,
and grass browns passin into cold winter,
Ain't no Aunt Sue's to read about harvest.
She's gone from the porches. The porches gone
from the neighborhoods, and the daddies left
with summer. Aunt Sue stayed behind, with child.
But Langston, ain't no stories left in her.
She done let the wood in her chair splinter
and the legs got loose. Her hair like old rope,
in two braids unkept under blue scarves: grey.
Ain't no Aunt Sue left in Aunt Sue because
her body tired. She make the home, wages,
her front porch covered with drifting orange,
rust, yellow, the yard unkept, unwanted.
Ain't no good stories in Aunt Sue no more.
Just blue stories bout travelin men, wanderin
eyes, screamin child, him leavin her alone.

Ballad For a Lost Songbird

I look for peace,

from a voice

too sad.

I find that peace

from a voice,

too sad.

However, peace

from a sad voice

hurts more.

What words to be said

to her?

The pain in her voice

bound to

Despair.

Sounds of muffled vocals,

muted brass,

distinct whistles

of birds

pass

into nothing.

Child in the Park,

seated, quiet:

Do you notice the people

walking through?

Do you notice how the planes

fly?

Do you notice how the birds

float to trees

at

dusk?

Home is close,

three blocks south,

somewhere --

that seems like

nowhere.

Keep On

Late evening playa
Big Pimpin
On the scene
Til early morn.

7 a.m.
his work time come
Big Pimpin
to doggone tired
his body worn

Perhaps

I questioned you love
you couldn't comprehend
Your eyes seemed uncertain
you tried to understand

Epilogue

Stories typically adhere to a format that allows for a manipulation of characters and situations. A story usually revolves about a central theme which allows the plot to develop. I have found that often, when you attempt to create a work of fiction, you find yourself hindered by questions of form. Do you use a first person or third person omniscient voice? Will you foreshadow what will come in the later chapters early in the book, or just before what you believe will be the climax? I recently began work on a novel and from the extensive amount of research and time I placed into understanding the era in which the novel is set, I found myself overcome by emotions that ranged from anger and frustration, to pride and happiness. I discovered a lot about what writing means to me. In an attempt to break myself out of a rather long writer's block, I began to write about anything that I thought of, an attempt at fighting my way out of a corner. Hence the choppiness of this work. I revised the poems and the flash fictions but, I felt that it was important to maintain the concept of addressing what I was trying to understand and comprehend in each section.

There are several instances within this text where the writing is rather ambiguous. This intentional attempt at blending a universal you with a direct audience you, for me, compliments the stream of consciousness in which the work was written. I decided that a definite justification of the you, or explanation of who I attempted to reach is rather unnecessary. As a matter of fact it is somewhat impossible because of the way the piece was created.

The most important writing I feel I have accomplished to date is contained in this mixture of poems and short stories all connected to a central idea. It is important because it was born of spontaneity and each line written is a genuine response to something I read, watched or experienced while researching. The idea is the struggle with one's muse, a struggle with one's conscience and the dedication to becoming a writer who wants to write passionately and effectively using every tool a writer has available to them. Each story is of a writer writing himself out of a block. With that said I will conclude with something that was said to me by a friend.

"A line that is written in perfect meter can be the most impassionate mix of words a writer may bring into existence. Yet a free verse line can erupt on the paper causing you to use each God given sense you have. This works both ways of course. A poem or story without form can, and will, elicit a response of disgust from a formalist, but it may be accepted as great by someone who simply enjoys the written word."

I tend to believe that you are not really striving to find the best writer you can be without studying and listening. Go figure.

This book is for you mom. 12 years in the making. Sept. 21, 2007